Algernon Charles Swinburne

The Tale of Balen

Algernon Charles Swinburne

The Tale of Balen

ISBN/EAN: 9783337074111

Printed in Europe, USA, Canada, Australia, Japan

Cover: Foto ©ninafisch / pixelio.de

More available books at **www.hansebooks.com**

THE TALE OF BALEN

BY

ALGERNON CHARLES SWINBURNE

LONDON
CHATTO & WINDUS, PICCADILLY
1896

DEDICATION.

TO MY MOTHER.

Love that holds life and death in fee,
Deep as the clear unsounded sea
And sweet as life or death can be,
Lays here my hope, my heart, and me
    Before you, silent, in a song.
Since the old wild tale, made new, found grace,
When half sung through, before your face,
It needs must live a springtide space,
    While April suns grow strong.

March 24, 1896.

THE
TALE OF BALEN

I

In hawthorn-time the heart grows light,

The world is sweet in sound and sight,

Glad thoughts and birds take flower and flight,

The heather kindles toward the light,

    The whin is frankincense and flame.

And be it for strife or be it for love

The falcon quickens as the dove

When earth is touched from heaven above

    With joy that knows no name.

And glad in spirit and sad in soul
With dream and doubt of days that roll
As waves that race and find no goal
Rode on by bush and brake and bole
    A northern child of earth and sea.
The pride of life before him lay
Radiant : the heavens of night and day
Shone less than shone before his way
    His ways and days to be.

And all his life of blood and breath
Sang out within him : time and death
Were even as words a dreamer saith
When sleep within him slackeneth,
    And light and life and spring were one.
The steed between his knees that sprang,
The moors and woods that shone and sang,
The hours wherethrough the spring's breath rang,
    Seemed ageless as the sun.

But alway through the bounteous bloom
That earth gives thanks if heaven illume
His soul forefelt a shadow of doom,
His heart foreknew a gloomier gloom
    Than closes all men's equal ways,
Albeit the spirit of life's light spring
With pride of heart upheld him, king
And lord of hours like snakes that sting
    And nights that darken days.

And as the strong spring round him grew
Stronger, and all blithe winds that blew
Blither, and flowers that flowered anew
More glad of sun and air and dew,
    The shadow lightened on his soul
And brightened into death and died
Like winter, as the bloom waxed wide
From woodside on to riverside
    And southward goal to goal.

Along the wandering ways of Tyne,
By beech and birch and thorn that shine
And laugh when life's requickening wine
Makes night and noon and dawn divine
    And stirs in all the veins of spring,
And past the brightening banks of Tees,
He rode as one that breathes and sees
A sun more blithe, a merrier breeze,
    A life that hails him king.

And down the softening south that knows
No more how glad the heather glows,
Nor how, when winter's clarion blows
Across the bright Northumbrian snows,
    Sea-mists from east and westward meet,
Past Avon senseless yet of song
And Thames that bore but swans in throng
He rode elate in heart and strong
    In trust of days as sweet.

So came he through to Camelot,

Glad, though for shame his heart waxed hot,

For hope within it withered not

To see the shaft it dreamed of shot

    Fair toward the glimmering goal of fame.

And all King Arthur's knightliest there

Approved him knightly, swift to dare

And keen to bid their records bear

    Sir Balen's northern name.

Sir Balen of Northumberland

Gat grace before the king to stand

High as his heart was, and his hand

Wrought honour toward the strange north strand

    That sent him south so goodly a knight.

And envy, sick with sense of sin,

Began as poisonous herbs begin

To work in base men's blood, akin

    To men's of nobler might.

And even so fell it that his doom,

For all his bright life's kindling bloom

And light that took no thought for gloom,

Fell as a breath from the opening tomb

  Full on him ere he wist or thought.

For once a churl of royal seed,

King Arthur's kinsman, faint in deed

And loud in word that knew not heed,

  Spake shame where shame was nought.

' What doth one here in Camelot

Whose birth was northward? Wot we not

As all his brethren borderers wot

How blind of heart, how keen and hot,

  The wild north lives and hates the south?

Men of the narrowing march that knows

Nought save the strength of storms and snows,

What would these carles where knighthood blows

  A trump of kinglike mouth?'

Swift from his place leapt Balen, smote
The liar across his face, and wrote
His wrath in blood upon the bloat
Brute cheek that challenged shame for note
    How vile a king-born knave might be.
Forth sprang their swords, and Balen slew
The knave ere well one witness knew
Of all that round them stood or drew
    What sight was there to see.

Then spake the great king's wrathful will
A doom for six dark months to fill
Wherein close prison held him, still
And steadfast-souled for good or ill.
    But when those weary days lay dead
His lordliest knights and barons spake
Before the king for Balen's sake
Good speech and wise, of force to break
    The bonds that bowed his head.

II

In linden-time the heart is high
For pride of summer passing by
With lordly laughter in her eye ;
A heavy splendour in the sky
    Uplifts and bows it down again.
The spring had waned from wood and wold
Since Balen left his prison hold
And lowlier-hearted than of old
    Beheld it wax and wane.

Though humble heart and poor array
Kept not from spirit and sense away
Their noble nature, nor could slay
The pride they bade but pause and stay
 Till time should bring its trust to flower,
Yet even for noble shame's sake, born
Of hope that smiled on hate and scorn,
He held him still as earth ere morn
 Ring forth her rapturous hour.

But even as earth when dawn takes flight
And beats her wings of dewy light
Full in the faltering face of night,
His soul awoke to claim by right
 The life and death of deed and doom,
When once before the king there came
A maiden clad with grief and shame
And anguish burning her like flame
 That feeds on flowers in bloom.

Beneath a royal mantle, fair
With goodly work of lustrous vair,
Girt fast against her side she bare
A sword whose weight bade all men there
    Quail to behold her face again.
Save of a passing perfect knight
Not great alone in force and fight
It might not be for any might
    Drawn forth, and end her pain.

So said she: then King Arthur spake:
'Albeit indeed I dare not take
Such praise on me, for knighthood's sake
And love of ladies will I make
    Assay if better none may be.'
By girdle and by sheath he caught
The sheathed and girded sword, and wrought
With strength whose force availed him nought
    To save and set her free.

Again she spake: 'No need to set
The might that man has matched not yet
Against it: he whose hand shall get
Grace to release the bonds that fret
 My bosom and my girdlestead
With little strain of strength or strife
Shall bring me as from death to life
And win to sister or to wife
 Fame that outlives men dead.'

Then bade the king his knights assay
This mystery that before him lay
And mocked his might of manhood. 'Nay,'
Quoth she, ' the man that takes away
 This burden laid on me must be
A knight of record clean and fair
As sunlight and the flowerful air,
By sire and mother born to bear
 A name to shame not me.'

Then forth strode Launcelot, and laid
The mighty-moulded hand that made
Strong knights reel back like birds affrayed
By storm that smote them as they strayed
    Against the hilt that yielded not.
Then Tristram, bright and sad and kind
As one that bore in noble mind
Love that made light as darkness blind,
    Fared even as Launcelot.

Then Lamoracke, with hardier cheer,
As one that held all hope and fear
Wherethrough the spirit of man may steer
In life and death less dark or dear,
    Laid hand thereon, and fared as they.
With half a smile his hand he drew
Back from the spell-bound thing, and threw
With half a glance his heart anew
    Toward no such blameless may.

Between Iseult and Guenevere

Sat one of name as high to hear,

But darklier doomed than they whose cheer

Foreshowed not yet the deadlier year

    That bids the queenliest head bow down,

The queen Morgause of Orkney : they

With scarce a flash of the eye could say

The very word of dawn, when day

    Gives earth and heaven their crown.

But bright and dark as night or noon

And lowering as a storm-flushed moon

When clouds and thwarting winds distune

The music of the midnight, soon

    To die from darkening star to star

And leave a silence in the skies

That yearns till dawn find voice and rise,

Shone strange as fate Morgause, with eyes

    That dwelt on days afar.

A glance that shot on Lamoracke
As from a storm-cloud bright and black
Fire swift and blind as death's own track
Turned fleet as flame on Arthur back
    From him whose hand forsook the hilt :
And one in blood and one in sin
Their hearts caught fire of pain within
And knew no goal for them to win
    But death that guerdons guilt.

Then Gawain, sweet of soul and gay
As April ere he dreams of May,
Strove, and prevailed not : then Sir Kay,
The snake-souled envier, vile as they
    That fawn and foam and lurk and lie,
Sire of the bastard band whose brood
Was alway found at servile feud
With honour, faint and false and lewd,
    Scarce grasped and put it by.

Then wept for woe the damsel bound
With iron and with anguish round,
That none to help her grief was found
Or loose the inextricably inwound
    Grim curse that girt her life with grief
And made a burden of her breath,
Harsh as the bitterness of death.
Then spake the king as one that saith
    Words bitterer even than brief.

' Methought the wide round world could bring
Before the face of queen or king
No knights more fit for fame to sing
Than fill this full Round Table's ring
    With honour higher than pride of place:
But now my heart is wrung to know,
Damsel, that none whom fame can show
Finds grace to heal or help thy woe:
    God gives them not the grace.'

Then from the lowliest place thereby,
With heart-enkindled cheek and eye
Most like the star and kindling sky
That say the sundawn's hour is high
　　When rapture trembles through the sea,
Strode Balen in his poor array
Forth, and took heart of grace to pray
The damsel suffer even him to assay
　　His power to set her free.

Nay, how should he avail, she said,
Averse with scorn-averted head,
Where these availed not? none had sped
Of all these mightier men that led
　　The lists wherein he might not ride,
And how should less men speed? But he,
With lordlier pride of courtesy,
Put forth his hand and set her free
　　From pain and humbled pride.

But on the sword he gazed elate
With hope set higher than fear or fate,
Or doubt of darkling days in wait;
And when her thankful praise waxed great
    And craved of him the sword again,
He would not give it. ' Nay, for mine
It is till force may make it thine.'
A smile that shone as death may shine
    Spake toward him bale and bane.

Strange lightning flickered from her eyes.
' Gentle and good in knightliest guise
And meet for quest of strange emprise
Thou hast here approved thee : yet not wise
    To keep the sword from me, I wis.
For with it thou shalt surely slay
Of all that look upon the day
The man best loved of thee, and lay
    Thine own life down for his.'

'What chance God sends, that chance I take,'
He said. Then soft and still she spake;
'I would but for thine only sake
Have back the sword of thee, and break
    The links of doom that bind thee round.
But seeing thou wilt not have it so,
My heart for thine is wrung with woe.'
'God's will,' quoth he, 'it is, we know,
    Wherewith our lives are bound.'

'Repent it must thou soon,' she said,
'Who wouldst not hear the rede I read
For thine and not for my sake, sped
In vain as waters heavenward shed
    From springs that falter and depart
Earthward. God bids not thee believe
Truth, and the web thy life must weave
For even this sword to close and cleave
    Hangs heavy round my heart.'

So passed she mourning forth.   But he,
With heart of springing hope set free
As birds that breast and brave the sea,
Bade horse and arms and armour be
    Made straightway ready toward the fray.
Nor even might Arthur's royal prayer
Withhold him, but with frank and fair
Thanksgiving and leave-taking there
    He turned him thence away.

III

As the east wind, when the morning's breast
Gleams like a bird's that leaves the nest,
A fledgeling halcyon's bound on quest,
Drives wave on wave on wave to west
    Till all the sea be life and light,
So time's mute breath, that brings to bloom
All flowers that strew the dead spring's tomb,
Drives day on day on day to doom
    Till all man's day be night.

THE TALE OF BALEN

Brief as the breaking of a wave

That hurls on man his thunderous grave

Ere fear find breath to cry or crave

Life that no chance may spare or save,

    The light of joy and glory shone

Even as in dreams where death seems dead

Round Balen's hope-exalted head,

Shone, passed, and lightened as it fled

    The shadow of doom thereon.

For as he bound him thence to fare,

Before the stately presence there

A lady like a windflower fair,

Girt on with raiment strange and rare

    That rippled whispering round her, came.

Her clear cold eyes, all glassy grey,

Seemed lit not with the light of day

But touched with gleams that waned away

    Of quelled and fading flame.

Before the king she bowed and spake:
'King, for thine old faith's plighted sake
To me the lady of the lake,
I come in trust of thee to take
  The guerdon of the gift I gave,
Thy sword Excalibur.'   And he
Made answer: 'Be it whate'er it be,
If mine to give, I give it thee,
  Nor need is thine to crave.'

As when a gleam of wicked light
Turns half a low-lying water bright
That moans beneath the shivering night
With sense of evil sound and sight
  And whispering witchcraft's bated breath,
Her wan face quickened as she said:
'This knight that won the sword—his head
I crave or hers that brought it.   Dead,
  Let these be one in death.'

' Not with mine honour this may be ;

Ask all save this thou wilt,' quoth he,

' And have thy full desire.'   But she

Made answer : ' Nought will I of thee,

 Nought if not this.'   Then Balen turned,

And saw the sorceress hard beside

By whose fell craft his mother died :

Three years he had sought her, and here espied

 His heart against her yearned.

' Ill be thou met,' he said, ' whose ire

Would slake with blood thy soul's desire :

By thee my mother died in fire ;

Die thou by me a death less dire.'

 Sharp flashed his sword forth, fleet as flame,

And shore away her sorcerous head.

' Alas for shame,' the high king said,

' That one found once my friend lies dead ;

 Alas for all our shame !

' Thou shouldst have here forborne her ; yea,
Were all the wrongs that bid men slay
Thine, heaped too high for wrath to weigh,
Not here before my face today
    Was thine the right to wreak thy wrong.'
Still stood he then as one that found
His rose of hope by storm discrowned,
And all the joy that girt him round
    Brief as a broken song.

Yet ere he passed he turned and spake:
' King, only for thy nobler sake
Than aught of power man's power may take
Or pride of place that pride may break
    I bid the lordlier man in thee,
That lives within the king, give ear.
This justice done before thee here
On one that hell's own heart holds dear,
    Needs might not this but be.

' Albeit, for all that pride would prove,

My heart be wrung to lose thy love,

It yet repents me not hereof:

So many an eagle and many a dove,

    So many a knight, so many a may,

This water-snake of poisonous tongue

To death by words and wiles hath stung,

That her their slayer, from hell's lake sprung,

    I did not ill to slay.'

'Yea,' said the king, 'too high of heart

To stand before a king thou art;

Yet irks it me to bid thee part

And take thy penance for thy part,

    That God may put upon thy pride.'

Then Balen took the severed head

And toward his hostry turned and sped

As one that knew not quick from dead

    Nor good from evil tide.

He bade his squire before him stand
And take that sanguine spoil in hand
And bear it far by shore and strand
Till all in glad Northumberland
    That loved him, seeing it, all might know
His deadliest foe was dead, and hear
How free from prison as from fear
He dwelt in trust of the answering year
    To bring him weal for woe.

'And tell them, now I take my way
To meet in battle, if I may,
King Ryons of North Wales, and slay
That king of kernes whose fiery sway
    Doth all the marches dire despite
That serve King Arthur: so shall he
Again be gracious lord to me,
And I that leave thee meet with thee
    Once more in Arthur's sight.'

So spake he ere they parted, nor
Took shame or fear to counsellor,
As one whom none laid ambush for ;
And wist not how Sir Launceor,
    The wild king's son of Ireland, hot
And high in wrath to know that one
Stood higher in fame before the sun,
Even Balen, since the sword was won,
    Drew nigh from Camelot.

For thence, in heat of hate and pride,
As one that man might bid not bide,
He craved the high king's grace to ride
On quest of Balen far and wide
    And wreak the wrong his wrath had wrought.
'Yea,' Arthur said, 'for such despite
Was done me never in my sight
As this thine hand shall now requite
    If trust avail us aught.'

But ere he passed, in eager mood
To feed his hate with bitter food,
Before the king's face Merlin stood
And heard his tale of ill and good,
    Of Balen, and the sword achieved,
And whence it smote as heaven's red ire
That direful dame of doom as dire;
And how the king's wrath turned to fire
    The grief wherewith he grieved.

And darkening as he gave it ear,
The still face of the sacred seer
Waxed wan with wrath and not with fear,
And ever changed its cloudier cheer
    Till all his face was very night.
' This damosel that brought the sword,'
He said, ' before the king my lord,
And all these knights about his board,
    Hath done them all despite.

THE TALE OF BALEN

' The falsest damosel she is

That works men ill on earth, I wis,

And all her mind is toward but this,

To kill as with a lying kiss

    Truth, and the life of noble trust.

A brother hath she,—see but now

The flame of shame that brands her brow!—

A true man, pure as faith's own vow,

    Whose honour knows not rust.

' This good knight found within her bower

A felon and her paramour,

And slew him in his shameful hour,

As right gave might and righteous power

    To hands that wreaked so foul a wrong.

Then, for the hate her heart put on,

She sought by ways where death had gone

The lady Lyle of Avalon,

    Whose crafts are strange and strong.

'The sorceress, one with her in thought,
Gave her that sword of magic, wrought
By charms whereof sweet heaven sees nought,
That hither girt on her she brought
 To be by doom her brother's bane.
And grief it is to think how he
That won it, being of heart so free
And perfect found in chivalry,
 Shall by that sword lie slain.

'Great pity it is and strange despite
That one whose eyes are stars to light
Honour, and shine as heaven's own height,
Should perish, being the goodliest knight
 That even the all-glorious north has borne.
Nor shall my lord the king behold
A lordlier friend of mightier mould
Than Balen, though his tale be told
 Ere noon fulfil his morn.'

IV

As morning hears before it run
The music of the mounting sun,
And laughs to watch his trophies won
From darkness, and her hosts undone,
    And all the night become a breath,
Nor dreams that fear should hear and flee
The summer menace of the sea,
So hears our hope what life may be,
    And knows it not for death.

Each day that slays its hours and dies
Weeps, laughs, and lightens on our eyes,
And sees and hears not: smiles and sighs
As flowers ephemeral fall and rise
    About its birth, about its way,
And pass as love and sorrow pass,
As shadows flashing down a glass,
As dew-flowers blowing in flowerless grass,
    As hope from yesterday.

The blossom of the sunny dew
That now the stronger sun strikes through
Fades off the blade whereon it blew
No fleetlier than the flowers that grew
    On hope's green stem in life's fierce light.
Nor might the glory soon to sit
Awhile on Balen's crest alit
Outshine the shadow of doom on it
    Or stay death's wings from flight.

Dawn on a golden moorland side

By holt and heath saw Balen ride

And Launceor after, pricked with pride

And stung with spurring envy : wide

    And far he had ridden athwart strange lands

And sought amiss the man he found

And cried on, till the stormy sound·

Rang as a rallying trumpet round

    That fires men's hearts and hands.

Abide he bade him : nor was need

To bid when Balen wheeled his steed

Fiercely, less fain by word than deed

To bid his envier evil speed,

    And cried, 'What wilt thou with me?' Loud

Rang Launceor's vehement answer : 'Knight,

To avenge on thee the dire despite

Thou hast done us all in Arthur's sight

    I stand toward Arthur vowed.'

'Ay?' Balen said: 'albeit I see
I needs must deal in strife with thee,
Light is the wyte thou layest on me;
For her I slew and sinned not, she
    Was dire in all men's eyes as death,
Or none were lother found than I
By me to bid a woman die:
As lief were loyal men to lie,
    Or scorn what honour saith.'

As the arched wave's weight against the reef
Hurls, and is hurled back like a leaf
Storm-shrivelled, and its rage of grief
Speaks all the loud broad sea in brief,
    And quells the hearkening hearts of men,
Or as the crash of overfalls
Down under blue smooth water brawls
Like jarring steel on ruining walls,
    So rang their meeting then.

As wave on wave shocks, and confounds
The bounding bulk whereon it bounds
And breaks and shattering seaward sounds
As crying of the old sea's wolves and hounds
    That moan and ravin and rage and wail,
So steed on steed encountering sheer
Shocked, and the strength of Launceor's spear
Shivered on Balen's shield, and fear
    Bade hope within him quail.

But Balen's spear through Launceor's shield
Clove as a ploughshare cleaves the field
And pierced the hauberk triple-steeled,
That horse with horseman stricken reeled,
    And as a storm-breached rock falls, fell.
And Balen turned his horse again
And wist not yet his foe lay slain,
And saw him dead that sought his bane
    And wrought and fared not well.

Suddenly, while he gazed and stood,
And mused in many-minded mood
If life or death were evil or good,
Forth of a covert of a wood
  That skirted half the moorland lea
Fast rode a maiden flower-like white
Full toward that fair wild place of fight,
Anhungered of the woful sight
  God gave her there to see.

And seeing the man there fallen and dead,
She cried against the sun that shed
Light on the living world, and said,
' O Balen, slayer whose hand is red,
  Two bodies and one heart thou hast slain,
Two hearts within one body: aye,
Two souls thou hast lost; by thee they die,
Cast out of sight of earth and sky
  And all that made them fain.'

And from the dead his sword she caught,

And fell in trance that wist of nought,

Swooning : but softly Balen sought

To win from her the sword she thought

    To die on, dying by Launceor's side.

Again her wakening wail outbroke

As wildly, sword in hand, she woke

And struck one swift and bitter stroke

    That healed her, and she died.

And sorrowing for their strange love's sake

Rode Balen forth by lawn and lake,

By moor and moss and briar and brake,

And in his heart their sorrow spake

    Whose lips were dumb as death, and said

Mute words of presage blind and vain

As rain-stars blurred and marred by rain

To wanderers on a moonless main

    Where night and day seem dead.

Then toward a sunbright wildwood side
He looked and saw beneath it ride
A knight whose arms afar espied
By note of name and proof of pride
    Bare witness of his brother born,
His brother Balan, hard at hand,
Twin flower of bright Northumberland,
Twin sea-bird of their loud sea-strand,
    Twin song-bird of their morn.

Ah then from Balen passed away
All dread of night, all doubt of day,
All care what life or death might say,
All thought of all worse months than May:
    Only the might of joy in love
Brake forth within him as a fire,
And deep delight in deep desire
Of far-flown days whose full-souled quire
    Rang round from the air above.

From choral earth and quiring air
Rang memories winged like songs that bear
Sweet gifts for spirit and sense to share:
For no man's life knows love more fair
    And fruitful of memorial things
Than this the deep dear love that breaks
With sense of life on life, and makes
The sundawn sunnier as it wakes
    Where morning round it rings.

'O brother, O my brother!' cried
Each upon each, and cast aside
Their helms unbraced that might not hide
From sight of memory single-eyed
    The likeness graven of face and face,
And kissed and wept upon each other
For joy and pity of either brother,
And love engraffed by sire and mother,
    God's natural gift of grace.

And each with each took counsel meet
For comfort, making sorrow sweet,
And grief a goodly thing to greet:
And word from word leapt light and fleet
    Till all the venturous tale was told,
And how in Balen's hope it lay
To meet the wild Welsh king and slay,
And win from Arthur back for pay
    The grace he gave of old.

'And thither will not thou with me
And win as great a grace for thee?'
'That will I well,' quoth Balan: 'we
Will cleave together, bound and free,
    As brethren should, being twain and one.'
But ere they parted thence there came
A creature withered as with flame,
A dwarf mismade in nature's shame,
    Between them and the sun.

And riding fleet as fire may glide
He found the dead lie side by side,
And wailed and rent his hair and cried,
'Who hath done this deed?' And Balen eyed
    The strange thing loathfully, and said,
'The knight I slew, who found him fain
And keen to slay me: seeing him slain,
The maid I sought to save in vain,
    Self-stricken, here lies dead.

'Sore grief was mine to see her die,
And for her true faith's sake shall I
Love, and with love of heart more high,
All women better till I die.'
    'Alas,' the dwarf said, 'ill for thee
In evil hour this deed was done:
For now the quest shall be begun
Against thee, from the dawning sun
    Even to the sunset sea.

'From shore to mountain, dawn to night,
The kinsfolk of this great dead knight
Will chase thee to thy death.'   A light
Of swift blithe scorn flashed answer bright
    As fire from Balen's eye.   'For that,
Small fear shall fret my heart,' quoth he:
'But that my lord the king should be
For this dead man's sake wroth with me,
    Weep might it well thereat.'

Then murmuring passed the dwarf away,
And toward the knights in fair array
Came riding eastward up the way
From where the flower-soft lowlands lay
    A king whose name the sweet south-west
Held high in honour, and the land
That bowed beneath his gentle hand
Wore on its wild bright northern strand
    Tintagel for a crest.

And Balen hailed with homage due

King Mark of Cornwall, when he knew

The pennon that before him flew :

And for those lovers dead and true

    The king made moan to hear their doom ;

And for their sorrow's sake he sware

To seek in all the marches there

The church that man might find most fair

    And build therein their tomb.

V

As thought from thought takes wing and flies,
As month on month with sunlit eyes
Tramples and triumphs in its rise,
As wave smites wave to death and dies,
    So chance on hurtling chance like steel
Strikes, flashes, and is quenched, ere fear
Can whisper hope, or hope can hear,
If sorrow or joy be far or near
    For time to hurt or heal.

Swift as a shadow and strange as light
That cleaves in twain the shadow of night
Before the wide-winged word takes flight
That thunder speaks to depth and height
    And quells the quiet hour with sound,
There came before King Mark and stood
Between the moorside and the wood
The man whose word God's will made good,
    Nor guile was in it found.

And Merlin said to Balen: 'Lo,
Thou hast wrought thyself a grievous woe
To let this lady die, and know
Thou mightst have stayed her deadly blow.'
    And Balen answered him and said,
'Nay, by my truth to faith, not I,
So fiercely fain she was to die;
Ere well her sword had flashed on high,
    Self-slain she lay there dead.'

Again and sadly Merlin spake:
'My heart is wrung for this deed's sake,
To know thee therefore doomed to take
Upon thine hand a curse, and make
    Three kingdoms pine through twelve years'
        change,
In want and woe: for thou shalt smite
The man most noble and truest knight
That looks upon the live world's light
    A dolorous stroke and strange.

'And not till years shall round their goal
May this man's wound thou hast given be whole.'
And Balen, stricken through the soul
By dark-winged words of doom and dole,
    Made answer: 'If I wist it were
No lie but sooth thou sayest of me,
Then even to make a liar of thee
Would I too slay myself, and see
    How death bids dead men fare.'

And Merlin took his leave and passed
And was not : and the shadow as fast
Went with him that his word had cast,
Too fleet for thought thereof to last :
 And there those brethren bade King Mark
Farewell : but fain would Mark have known
The strong knight's name who had overthrown
The pride of Launceor, when it shone
 Bright as it now lay dark.

And Balan for his brother spake,
Saying : ' Sir, albeit him list not break
The seal of secret time, nor shake
Night off him ere his morning wake,
 By these two swords he is girt withal
May men that praise him, knights and lords,
Call him the knight that bears two swords,
And all the praise his fame accords
 Make answer when they call.'

So parted they toward eventide ;
And tender twilight, heavy-eyed,
Saw deep down glimmering woodlands ride
Balen and Balan side by side,
 Till where the leaves grew dense and dim
Again they spied from far draw near
The presence of the sacred seer,
But so disguised and strange of cheer
 That seeing they knew not him.

' Now whither ride ye,' Merlin said,
' Through shadows that the sun strikes red,
Ere night be born or day be dead ? '
But they, for doubt half touched with dread,
 Would say not where their goal might lie.
' And thou,' said Balen, ' what art thou,
To walk with shrouded eye and brow ? '
He said : ' Me lists not show thee now
 By name what man am I.'

'Ill seen is this of thee,' said they,

'That thou art true in word and way

Nor fain to fear the face of day,

Who wilt not as a true man say

    The name it shames not him to bear.'

He answered: 'Be it or be it not so,

Yet why ye ride this way I know,

To meet King Ryons as a foe,

    And how your hope shall fare.

'Well, if ye hearken toward my rede,

Ill, if ye hear not, shall ye speed.'

'Ah, now,' they cried, 'thou art ours at need:

What Merlin saith we are fain to heed.'

    'Great worship shall ye win,' said he,

'And look that ye do knightly now,

For great shall be your need, I trow.'

And Balen smiled: 'By knighthood's vow,

    The best we may will we.'

Then Merlin bade them turn and take
Rest, for their good steeds' weary sake,
Between the highway and the brake,
Till starry midnight bade them wake :
    Then ' Rise,' he said, ' the king is nigh,
Who hath stolen from all his host away
With threescore horse in armed array,
The goodliest knights that bear his sway
    And hold his kingdom high.

' And twenty ride of them before
To bear his errand, ere the door
Turn of the night, sealed fast no more,
And sundawn bid the stars wax hoar ;
    For by the starshine of to-night
He seeks a leman where she waits
His coming, dark and swift as fate's,
And hearkens toward the unopening gates
    That yield not him to sight.

Then through the glimmering gloom around

A shadowy sense of light and sound

Made, ere the proof thereof were found,

The brave blithe hearts within them bound,

    And 'Where,' quoth Balen, 'rides the king?'

But softer spake the seer : ' Abide,

Till hither toward your spears he ride,

Where all the narrowing woodland side

    Grows dense with boughs that cling.'

There in that straitening way they met

The wild Welsh host against them set,

And smote their strong king down, ere yet

His hurrying horde of spears might get

    Fierce vantage of them. Then the fight

Grew great and joyous as it grew,

For left and right those brethren slew,

Till all the lawn waxed red with dew

    More deep than dews of night.

And ere the full fierce tale was read
Full forty lay before them dead,
And fast the hurtling remnant fled
And wist not whither fear had led :
    And toward the king they went again,
And would have slain him : but he bowed
Before them, crying in fear aloud
For grace they gave him, seeing the proud
    Wild king brought lowest of men.

And ere the wildwood leaves were stirred
With song or wing of wakening bird,
In Camelot was Merlin's word
With joy in joyous wonder heard
    That told of Arthur's bitterest foe
Diskingdomed and discomfited.
'By whom?' the high king smiled and said.
He answered : 'Ere the dawn wax red,
    To-morrow bids you know.

'Two knights whose heart and hope are one
And fain to win your grace have done
This work whereby if grace be won
Their hearts shall hail the enkindling sun
  With joy more keen and deep than day.'
And ere the sundawn drank the dew
Those brethren with their prisoner drew
To the outer guard they gave him to
  And passed again away.

And Arthur came as toward his guest
To greet his foe, and bade him rest
As one returned from nobler quest
And welcome from the stormbright west,
  But by what chance he fain would hear.
'The chance was hard and strange, sir king,'
Quoth Ryons, bowed in thanksgiving.
'Who won you?' Arthur said: 'the thing
  Is worth a warrior's ear.'

The wild king flushed with pride and shame,
Answering : 'I know not either name
Of those that there against us came
And withered all our strength like flame :
 The knight that bears two swords is one,
And one his brother : not on earth
May men meet men of knightlier worth
Nor mightier born of mortal birth
 That hail the sovereign sun.'

And Arthur said : 'I know them not ;
But much am I for this, God wot,
Beholden to them : Launcelot
Nor Tristram, when the war waxed hot
 Along the marches east and west,
Wrought ever nobler work than this.'
'Ah,' Merlin said, 'sore pity it is
And strange mischance of doom, I wis,
 That death should mar their quest.

' Balen, the perfect knight that won
The sword whose name is malison,
And made his deed his doom, is one:
Nor hath his brother Balan done
    Less royal service: not on earth
Lives there a nobler knight, more strong
Of soul to win men's praise in song,
Albeit the light abide not long
    That lightened round his birth.

' Yea, and of all sad things I know
The heaviest and the highest in woe
Is this, the doom whose date brings low
Too soon in timeless overthrow
    A head so high, a hope so sure.
The greatest moan for any knight
That ever won fair fame in fight
Shall be for Balen, seeing his might
    Must now not long endure.'

'Alas,' King Arthur said, 'he hath shown
Such love to me-ward that the moan
Made of him should be mine alone
Above all other, knowing it known
 I have ill deserved it of him.' 'Nay,'
Said Merlin, 'he shall do for you
Much more, when time shall be anew,
Than time hath given him chance to do
 Or hope may think to say.

'But now must be your powers purveyed
To meet, ere noon of morn be made
To-morrow, all the host arrayed
Of this wild foe's wild brother, laid
 Around against you: see to it well,
For now I part from you.' And soon,
When sundawn slew the withering moon,
Two hosts were met to win the boon
 Whose tale is death's to tell.

A lordly tale of knights and lords

For death to tell by count of swords

When war's wild harp in all its chords

Rang royal triumph, and the hordes

    Of hurtling foemen rocked and reeled

As waves wind-thwarted on the sea,

Was told of all that there might be,

Till scarce might battle hear or see

    The fortune of the field.

And many a knight won fame that day

When even the serpent soul of Kay

Was kindled toward the fiery play

As might a lion's be for prey,

    And won him fame that might not die

With passing of his rancorous breath

But clung about his life and death

As fire that speaks in cloud, and saith

    What strong men hear and fly.

And glorious works were Arthur's there,
That lit the battle-darkened air:
But when they saw before them fare
Like stars of storm the knight that bare
  Two swords about him girt for fray,
Balen, and Balan with him, then
Strong wonder smote the souls of men
If heaven's own host or hell's deep den
  Had sent them forth to slay.

So keen they rode across the fight,
So sharp they smote to left and right,
And made of hurtling darkness light
With lightning of their swords, till flight
  And fear before them flew like flame,
That Arthur's self had never known,
He said, since first his blast was blown,
Such lords of war as these alone
  That whence he knew not came.

But while the fire of war waxed hot
The wild king hearkened, hearing not,
Through storm of spears and arrow-shot,
For succour toward him from King Lot
    And all his host of sea-born men,
Strong as the strong storm-baffling bird
Whose cry round Orkney's headlands heard
Is as the sea's own sovereign word
    That mocks our mortal ken.

For Merlin's craft of prophecy,
Who wist that one of twain must die,
Put might in him to say thereby
Which head should lose its crown, and lie
    Stricken, though loth he were to know
That either life should wane and fail;
Yet most might Arthur's love avail,
And still with subtly tempered tale
    His wile held fast the foe.

With woven words of magic might
Wherein the subtle shadow and light
Changed hope and fear till fear took flight,
He stayed King Lot's fierce lust of fight
    Till all the wild Welsh war was driven
As foam before the wind that wakes
With the all-awakening sun, and breaks
Strong ships that rue the mirth it makes
    When grace to slay is given.

And ever hotter lit and higher,
As fire that meets encountering fire,
Waxed in King Lot his keen desire
To bid revenge within him tire
    On Arthur's ravaged fame and life:
Across the waves of war between
Floated and flashed, unseen and seen,
The lustrous likeness of the queen
    Whom shame had sealed his wife.

But when the woful word was brought
That while he tarried, doubting nought,
The hope was lost whose goal he sought
And all the fight he yearned for fought,
    His heart was rent for grief and shame,
And half his hope was set on flight
Till word was given him of a knight
Who said : ' They are weary and worn with fight,
    And we more fresh than flame.'

And bright and dark as night and day
Ere either find the unopening way
Clear, and forego the unaltering sway,
The sad king's face shone, frowning : ' Yea,
    I would that every knight of mine
Would do his part as I shall do,'
He said, ' till death or life anew
Shall judge between us as is due
    With wiser doom than thine.'

Then thundered all the awakening field
With crash of hosts that clashed and reeled,
Banner to banner, shield to shield,
And spear to splintering spear-shaft, steeled
 As heart against high heart of man,
As hope against high hope of knight
To pluck the crest and crown of fight
From war's clenched hand by storm's wild light,
 For blessing given or ban.

All hearts of hearkening men that heard
The ban twin-born with blessing, stirred
Like springtide waters, knew the word
Whereby the steeds of storm are spurred
 With ravenous rapture to destroy,
And laughed for love of battle, pierced
With passion of tempestuous thirst
And hungering hope to assuage it first
 With draughts of stormy joy.

But sheer ahead of the iron tide
That rocked and roared from side to side
Rode as the lightning's lord might ride
King Lot, whose heart was set to abide
    All peril of the raging hour,
And all his host of warriors born
Where lands by warring seas are worn
Was only by his hands upborne
    Who gave them pride and power.

But as the sea's hand smites the shore
And shatters all the strengths that bore
The ravage earth may bear no more,
So smote the hand of Pellinore
    Charging, a knight of Arthur's chief,
And clove his strong steed's neck in twain,
And smote him sheer through brow and brain,
Falling : and there King Lot lay slain,
    And knew not wrath or grief.

And all the host of Orkney fled,
And many a mother's son lay dead :
But when they raised the stricken head
Whence pride and power and shame were fled
  And rage and anguish now cast out,
And bore it toward a kingly tomb,
The wife whose love had wrought his doom
Came thither, fair as morning's bloom
  And dark as twilight's doubt.

And there her four strong sons and his,
Gawain and Gareth, Gaherys
And Agravain, whose sword's sharp kiss
With sound of hell's own serpent's hiss
  Should one day turn her life to death,
Stood mourning with her : but by these
Seeing Mordred as a seer that sees,
Anguish of terror bent her knees
  And caught her shuddering breath.

The splendour of her sovereign eyes
Flashed darkness deeper than the skies
Feel or fear when the sunset dies
On his that felt as midnight rise
    Their doom upon them, there undone
By faith in fear ere thought could yield
A shadowy sense of days revealed,
The ravin of the final field,
    The terror of their son.

For Arthur's, as they caught the light
That sought and durst not seek his sight,
Darkened, and all his spirit's might
Withered within him even as night
    Withers when sunrise thrills the sea.
But Mordred's lightened as with fire
That smote his mother and his sire
With darkling doom and deep desire
    That bade its darkness be.

And heavier on their hearts the weight
Sank of the fear that brings forth fate,
The bitter doubt whose womb is great
With all the grief and love and hate
    That turn to fire men's days on earth.
And glorious was the funeral made,
And dark the deepening dread that swayed
Their darkening souls whose light grew shade
    With sense of death in birth.

THE TALE OF BALEN

VI

In autumn, when the wind and sea
Rejoice to live and laugh to be,
And scarce the blast that curbs the tree
And bids before it quail and flee
    The fiery foliage, where its brand
Is radiant as the seal of spring,
Sounds less delight, and waves a wing
Less lustrous, life's loud thanksgiving
    Puts life in sea and land.

High hope in Balen's heart alight
Laughed, as from all that clamorous fight
He passed and sought not Arthur's sight,
Who fain had found his kingliest knight
    And made amend for Balen's wrong.
But Merlin gave his soul to see
Fate, rising as a shoreward sea,
And all the sorrow that should be
    Ere hope or fear thought long.

'O where are they whose hands upbore
My battle,' Arthur said, 'before
The wild Welsh host's wide rage and roar?
Balen and Balan, Pellinore,
    Where are they?' Merlin answered him:
'Balen shall be not long away
From sight of you, but night nor day
Shall bring his brother back to say
    If life burn bright or dim.'

'Now, by my faith,' said Arthur then,
'Two marvellous knights are they, whose ken
Toward battle makes the twain as ten,
And Balen most of all born men
    Passeth of prowess all I know
Or ever found or sought to see :
Would God he would abide with me,
To face the times foretold of thee
    And all the latter woe.'

For there had Merlin shown the king
The doom that songs unborn should sing,
The gifts that time should rise and bring
Of blithe and bitter days to spring
    As weeds and flowers against the sun.
And on the king for fear's sake fell
Sickness, and sorrow deep as hell,
Nor even might sleep bid fear farewell
    If grace to sleep were won.

Down in a meadow green and still
He bade the folk that wrought his will
Pitch his pavilion, where the chill
Soft night would let not rest fulfil
  His heart wherein dark fears lay deep.
And sharp against his hearing cast
Came a sound as of horsehoofs fast
Passing, that ere their sound were past
  Aroused him as from sleep.

And forth he looked along the grass
And saw before his portal pass
A knight that wailed aloud, ' Alas
That life should find this dolorous pass
  And find no shield from doom and dole ! '
And hearing all his moan, ' Abide,
Fair sir,' the king arose and cried,
' And say what sorrow bids you ride
  So sorrowful of soul.'

'My hurt may no man heal, God wot,
And help of man may speed me not,'
The sad knight said, 'nor change my lot.'
And toward the castle of Melyot
    Whose towers arose a league away
He passed forth sorrowing : and anon,
Ere well the woful sight were gone,
Came Balen down the meads that shone,
    Strong, bright, and brave as day.

And seeing the king there stand, the knight
Drew rein before his face to alight
In reverence made for love's sake bright
With joy that set his face alight
    As theirs who see, alive, above,
The sovereign of their souls, whose name
To them is even as love's own flame
To enkindle hope that heeds not fame
    And knows no lord but love.

And Arthur smiled on him, and said,
'Right welcome be thou: by my head,
I would not wish me better sped.
For even but now there came and fled
    Before me like a cloud that flies
A knight that made most heavy cheer,
I know not wherefore; nor may fear
Or pity give my heart to hear
    Or lighten on mine eyes.

'But even for fear's and pity's sake
Fain were I thou shouldst overtake
And fetch again this knight that spake
No word of answering grace to make
    Reply to mine that hailed him: thou,
By force or by goodwill, shalt bring
His face before me.' 'Yea, my king,'
Quoth Balen, 'and a greater thing
    Were less than is my vow.

THE TALE OF BALEN

'I would the task required and heard

Were heavier than your sovereign word

Hath laid on me:' and thence he spurred

Elate at heart as youth, and stirred

    With hope as blithe as fires a boy:

And many a mile he rode, and found

Far in a forest's glimmering bound

The man he sought afar around

    And seeing took fire for joy.

And with him went a maiden, fair

As flowers aflush with April air.

And Balen bade him turn him there

To tell the king what woes they were

    That bowed him down so sore: and he

Made woeful answer: 'This should do

Great scathe to me, with nought for you

Of help that hope might hearken to

    For boot that may not be.'

And Balen answered: 'I were loth
To fight as one perforce made wroth
With one that owes by knighthood's oath
One love, one service, and one troth
    With me to him whose gracious hand
Holds fast the helm of knighthood here
Whereby man's hope and heart may steer:
I pray you let not sorrow or fear
    Against his bidding stand.'

The strange knight gazed on him, and spake:
'Will you, for Arthur's royal sake,
Be warrant for me that I take
No scathe from strife that man may make?
    Then will I go with you.' And he
Made joyous answer: 'Yea, for I
Will be your warrant or will die.'
And thence they rode with hearts as high
    As men's that search the sea.

And as by noon's large light the twain
Before the tented hall drew rein,
Suddenly fell the strange knight, slain
By one that came and went again
    And none might see him ; but his spear
Clove through the body, swift as fire,
The man whose doom, forefelt as dire,
Had darkened all his life's desire,
    As one that death held dear.

And dying he turned his face and said,
' Lo now thy warrant that my head
Should fall not, following forth where led
A knight whose pledge hath left me dead.
    This darkling manslayer hath to name
Garlon : take thou my goodlier steed,
Seeing thine is less of strength and speed,
And ride, if thou be knight indeed,
    Even thither whence we came.

'And as the maiden's fair behest
Shall bid you follow on my quest,
Follow: and when God's will sees best,
Revenge my death, and let me rest
 As one that lived and died a knight,
Unstained of shame alive or dead.'
And Balen, wrung with sorrow, said,
'That shall I do: my hand and head
 I pledge to do you right.'

And thence with sorrowing heart and cheer
He rode, in grief that cast out fear
Lest death in darkness yet were near,
And bore the truncheon of the spear
 Wherewith the woful knight lay slain
To her with whom he rode, and she
Still bare it with her, fain to see
What righteous doom of God's might be
 The darkling manslayer's bane.

And down a dim deep woodland way
They rode between the boughs asway
With flickering winds whose flash and play
Made sunlight sunnier where the day
    Laughed, leapt, and fluttered like a bird
Caught in a light loose leafy net
That earth for amorous heaven had set
To hold and see the sundawn yet
    And hear what morning heard.

There in the sweet soft shifting light
Across their passage rode a knight
Flushed hot from hunting as from fight,
And seeing the sorrow-stricken sight
    Made question of them why they rode
As mourners sick at heart and sad,
When all alive about them bade
Sweet earth for heaven's sweet sake be glad
    As heaven for earth's love glowed.

' Me lists not tell you,' Balen said.
The strange knight's face grew keen and red;
' Now, might my hand but keep my head,
Even here should one of twain lie dead
    Were he no better armed than I.'
And Balen spake with smiling speed,
Where scorn and courtesy kept heed
Of either : ' That should little need :
    Not here shall either die.'

And all the cause he told him through
As one that feared not though he knew
All : and the strange knight spake anew,
Saying : ' I will part no more from you
    While life shall last me.' So they went
Where he might arm himself to ride,
And rode across wild ways and wide
To where against a churchyard side
    A hermit's harbour leant.

And there against them riding came
Fleet as the lightning's laugh and flame
The invisible evil, even the same
They sought and might not curse by name
    As hell's foul child on earth set free,
And smote the strange knight through, and fled,
And left the mourners by the dead.
'Alas, again,' Sir Balen said,
    'This wrong he hath done to me.'

And there they laid their dead to sleep
Royally, lying where wild winds keep
Keen watch and wail more soft and deep
Than where men's choirs bid music weep
    And song like incense heave and swell.
And forth again they rode, and found
Before them, dire in sight and sound,
A castle girt about and bound
    With sorrow like a spell.

Above it seemed the sun at noon
Sad as a wintry withering moon
That shudders while the waste wind's tune
Craves ever none may guess what boon,
    But all may know the boon for dire.
And evening on its darkness fell
More dark than very death's farewell,
And night about it hung like hell,
    Whose fume the dawn made fire.

And Balen lighted down and passed
Within the gateway, whence no blast
Rang as the sheer portcullis, cast
Suddenly down, fell, and made fast
    The gate behind him, whence he spied
A sudden rage of men without
And ravin of a murderous rout
That girt the maiden hard about
    With death on either side.

And seeing that shame and peril, fear
Bade wrath and grief awake and hear
What shame should say in fame's wide ear
If she, by sorrow sealed more dear
 Than joy might make her, so should die:
And up the tower's curled stair he sprang
As one that flies death's deadliest fang,
And leapt right out amid their gang
 As fire from heaven on high.

And they thereunder seeing the knight
Unhurt among their press alight
And bare his sword for chance of fight
Stood from him, loth to strive or smite,
 And bade him hear their woful word,
That not the maiden's death they sought;
But there through years too dire for thought
Had lain their lady stricken, and nought
 Might heal her: and he heard.

For there a maiden clean and whole
In virgin body and virgin soul,
Whose name was writ on royal roll,
That would but stain a silver bowl
    With offering of her stainless blood,
Therewith might heal her : so they stayed
For hope's sad sake each blameless maid
There journeying in that dolorous shade
    Whose bloom was bright in bud.

No hurt nor harm to her it were
If she should yield a sister there
Some tribute of her blood, and fare
Forth with this joy at heart to bear,
    That all unhurt and unafraid
This grace she had here by God's grace wrought.
And kindling all with kindly thought
And love that saw save love's self nought,
    Shone, smiled, and spake the maid.

'Good knight of mine, good will have I
To help this healing though I die.'
' Nay,' Balen said, ' but love may try
What help in living love may lie.
　—I will not lose the life of her
While my life lasteth.'   So she gave
The tribute love was fain to crave,
But might not heal though fain to save,
　Were God's grace helpfuller.

Another maid in later Mays
Won with her life that woful praise,
And died.   But they, when surging day's
Deep tide fulfilled the dawn's wide ways,
　Rode forth, and found by day or night
No chance to cross their wayfaring
Till when they saw the fourth day spring
A knight's hall gave them harbouring
　Rich as a king's house might.

And while they sat at meat and spake
Words bright and kind as grace might make
Sweet for true knighthood's kindly sake,
They heard a cry beside them break
    The still-souled joy of blameless rest.
'What noise is this?' quoth Balen. 'Nay,'
His knightly host made answer, ' may
Our grief not grieve you though I say
    How here I dwell unblest.

'Not many a day has lived and died
Since at a tournay late I tried
My strength to smite and turn and ride
Against a knight of kinglike pride,
    King Pellam's brother: twice I smote
The splendour of his strength to dust:
And he, fulfilled of hate's fierce lust,
Swore vengeance, pledged for hell to trust,
    And keen as hell's wide throat.

' Invisible as the spirit of night

That heaven and earth in depth and height

May see not by the mild moon's light

Nor even when stars would grant them sight,

 He walks and slays as plague's blind breath

Slays : and my son, whose anguish here

Makes moan perforce that mars our cheer,

He wounded, even ere love might fear

 That hate were strong as death.

' Nor may my son be whole till he

Whose stroke through him hath stricken me

Shall give again his blood to be

Our healing : yet may no man see

 This felon, clothed with darkness round

And keen as lightning's life.' Thereon

Spake Balen, and his presence shone

Even as the sun's when stars are gone

 That hear dawn's trumpet sound.

'That knight I know: two knights of mine,
Two comrades, sealed by faith's bright sign,
Whose eyes as ours that live should shine,
And drink the golden sunlight's wine
 With joy's thanksgiving that they live,
He hath slain in even the same blind wise:
Were all wide wealth beneath the skies
Mine, might I meet him, eyes on eyes,
 All would I laugh to give.'

His host made answer, and his gaze
Grew bright with trust as dawn's moist maze
With fire: 'Within these twenty days,
King Pellam, lord of Lystenayse,
 Holds feast through all this country cried,
And there before the knightly king
May no knight come except he bring
For witness of his wayfaring
 His paramour or bride.

'And there that day, so soon to shine,

This knight, your felon foe and mine,

Shall show, full-flushed with bloodred wine,

The fierce false face whereon we pine

 To wreak the wrong he hath wrought us, bare

As shame should see and brand it.' 'Then,'

Said Balen, 'shall he give again

His blood to heal your son, and men

 Shall see death blind him there.'

'Forth will we fare to-morrow,' said

His host: and forth, as sunrise led,

They rode; and fifteen days were fled

Ere toward their goal their steeds had sped.

 And there alighting might they find

For Balen's host no place to rest,

Who came without a gentler guest

Beside him: and that household's hest

 Bade leave his sword behind.

'Nay,' Balen said, 'that do I not:
My country's custom stands, God wot,
That none whose lot is knighthood's lot,
To ride where chance as fire is hot
  With hope or promise given of fight,
Shall fail to keep, for knighthood's part,
His weapon with him as his heart;
And as I came will I depart,
  Or hold herein my right.'

Then gat he leave to wear his sword
Beside the strange king's festal board
Where feasted many a knight and lord
In seemliness of fair accord:
  And Balen asked of one beside,
'Is there not in this court, if fame
Keep faith, a knight that hath to name
Garlon?' and saying that word of shame,
  He scanned that place of pride.

'Yonder he goeth against the light,
He with the face as swart as night,'
Quoth the other : ' but he rides to fight
Hid round by charms from all men's sight,
    And many a noble knight he hath slain,
Being wrapt in darkness deep as hell
And silence dark as shame.' 'Ah, well,'
Said Balen, ' is that he? the spell
    May be the sorcerer's bane.'

Then Balen gazed upon him long,
And thought, 'If here I wreak my wrong,
Alive I may not scape, so strong
The felon's friends about him throng ;
    And if I leave him here alive,
This chance perchance may life not give
Again : much evil, if he live,
He needs must do, should fear forgive
    When wrongs bid strike and strive.'

And Garlon, seeing how Balen's eye
Dwelt on him as his heart waxed high
With joy in wrath to see him nigh,
Rose wolf-like with a wolfish cry
  And crossed and smote him on the face,
Saying, 'Knight, what wouldst thou with me?
  Eat,
For shame, and gaze not: eat thy meat:
Do that thou art come for: stands thy seat
  Next ours of royal race?'

'Well hast thou said: thy rede rings true;
That which I came for will I do,'
Quoth Balen: forth his fleet sword flew,
And clove the head of Garlon through
  Clean to the shoulders. Then he cried
Loud to his lady, 'Give me here
The truncheon of the shameful spear
Wherewith he slew your knight, when fear
  Bade hate in darkness ride.'

And gladly, bright with grief made glad,
She gave the truncheon as he bade,
For still she bare it with her, sad
And strong in hopeless hope she had,
    Through all dark days of thwarting fear,
To see if doom should fall aright
And as God's fire-fraught thunder smite
That head, clothed round with hell-faced night,
    Bare now before her here.

And Balen smote therewith the dead
Dark felon's body through, and said
Aloud, 'With even this truncheon, red
With baser blood than brave men bled
    Whom in thy shameful hand it slew,
Thou hast slain a nobler knight, and now
It clings and cleaves thy body : thou
Shall cleave again no brave man's brow,
    Though hell would aid anew.'

And toward his host he turned and spake ;
' Now for your son's long-suffering sake
Blood ye may fetch enough, and take
Wherewith to heal his hurt, and make
    Death warm as life.'   Then rose a cry
Loud as the wind's when stormy spring
Makes all the woodland rage and ring :
' Thou hast slain my brother,' said the king,
    ' And here with him shalt die.'

' Ay ? ' Balen laughed him answer.   ' Well,
Do it then thyself.'   And the answer fell
Fierce as a blast of hate from hell,
' No man of mine that with me dwell
    Shall strike at thee but I their lord
For love of this my brother slain.'
And Pellam caught and grasped amain
A grim great weapon, fierce and fain
    To feed his hungering sword.

And eagerly he smote, and sped
Not well: for Balen's blade, yet red
With lifeblood of the murderous dead,
Between the swordstroke and his head
    Shone, and the strength of the eager stroke
Shore it in sunder: then the knight,
Naked and weaponless for fight,
Ran seeking him a sword to smite
    As hope within him woke.

And so their flight for deathward fast
From chamber forth to chamber passed
Where lay no weapon, till the last
Whose doors made way for Balen cast
    Upon him as a sudden spell
Wonder that even as lightning leapt
Across his heart and eyes, and swept
As storm across his soul that kept
    Wild watch, and watched not well.

For there the deed he did, being near
Death's danger, breathless as the deer
Driven hard to bay, but void of fear,
Brought sorrow down for many a year
    On many a man in many a land.
All glorious shone that chamber, bright
As burns at sunrise heaven's own height:
With cloth of gold the bed was dight,
    That flamed on either hand.

And one he saw within it lie:
A table of all clear gold thereby
Stood stately, fair as morning's eye,
With four strong silver pillars, high
    And firm as faith and hope may be:
And on it shone the gift he sought,
A spear most marvellously wrought,
That when his eye and handgrip caught
    Small fear at heart had he.

Right on King Pellam then, as fire
Turns when the thwarting winds wax higher,
He turned, and smote him down.   So dire
The stroke was, when his heart's desire
    Struck, and had all its fill of hate,
That as the king fell swooning down
Fell the walls, rent from base to crown,
Prone as prone seas that break and drown
    Ships fraught with doom for freight.

And there for three days' silent space
Balen and Pellam face to face
Lay dead or deathlike, and the place
Was death's blind kingdom, till the grace
    That God had given the sacred seer
For counsel or for comfort led
His Merlin thither, and he said,
Standing between the quick and dead,
    'Rise up, and rest not here.'

And Balen rose and set his eyes
Against the seer's as one that tries
His heart against the sea's and sky's
And fears not if he lives or dies,
 Saying, ' I would have my damosel,
Ere I fare forth, to fare with me.'
And sadly Merlin answered, ' See
Where now she lies ; death knows if she
 Shall now fare ill or well.

' And in this world we meet no more,
Balen.' And Balen, sorrowing sore,
Though fearless yet the heart he bore
Beat toward the life that lay before,
 Rode forth through many a wild waste land
Where men cried out against him, mad
With grievous faith in fear that bade
Their wrath make moan for doubt they had
 Lest hell had armed his hand.

For in that chamber's wondrous shrine
Was part of Christ's own blood, the wine
Shed of the true triumphal vine
Whose growth bids earth's deep darkness shine
 As heaven's deep light through the air and sea ;
That mystery toward our northern shore
Arimathean Joseph bore
For healing of our sins of yore,
 That grace even there might be.

And with that spear there shrined apart
Was Christ's side smitten to the heart.
And fiercer than the lightning's dart
The stroke was, and the deathlike smart
 Wherewith, nigh drained of blood and breath,
The king lay stricken as one long dead :
And Joseph's was the blood there shed,
For near akin was he that bled,
 Near even as life to death.

And therefore fell on all that land
Sorrow : for still on either hand,
As Balen rode alone and scanned
Bright fields and cities built to stand
    Till time should break them, dead men lay ;
And loud and long from all their folk
Living, one cry that cursed him broke ;
Three countries had his dolorous stroke
    Slain, or should surely slay.

VII

In winter, when the year burns low
As fire wherein no firebrands glow,
And winds dishevel as they blow
The lovely stormy wings of snow,
    The hearts of northern men burn bright
With joy that mocks the joy of spring
To hear all heaven's keen clarions ring
Music that bids the spirit sing
    And day give thanks for night.

Aloud and dark as hell or hate
Round Balen's head the wind of fate
Blew storm and cloud from death's wide gate:
But joy as grief in him was great
    To face God's doom and live or die,
Sorrowing for ill wrought unaware,
Rejoicing in desire to dare
All ill that innocence might bear
    With changeless heart and eye.

Yet passing fain he was when past
Those lands and woes at length and last.
Eight times, as thence he fared forth fast,
Dawn rose and even was overcast
    With starry darkness dear as day,
Before his venturous quest might meet
Adventure, seeing within a sweet
Green low-lying forest, hushed in heat,
    A tower that barred his way.

Strong summer, dumb with rapture, bound
With golden calm the woodlands round
Wherethrough the knight forth faring found
A knight that on the greenwood ground
  Sat mourning: fair he was to see,
And moulded as for love or fight
A maiden's dreams might frame her knight;
But sad in joy's far-flowering sight
  As grief's blind thrall might be.

'God save you,' Balen softly said,
'What grief bows down your heart and head
Thus, as one sorrowing for his dead?
Tell me, if haply I may stead
  In aught your sorrow, that I may.'
'Sir knight,' that other said, 'thy word
Makes my grief heavier that I heard.'
And pity and wonder inly stirred
  Drew Balen thence away.

And so withdrawn with silent speed

He saw the sad knight's stately steed,

A war-horse meet for warrior's need,

That none who passed might choose but heed,

 So strong he stood, so great, so fair,

With eyes afire for flight or fight,

A joy to look on, mild in might,

And swift and keen and kind as light,

 And all as clear of care.

And Balen, gazing on him, heard

Again his master's woful word

Sound sorrow through the calm unstirred

By fluttering wind or flickering bird,

 Thus: 'Ah, fair lady and faithless, why

Break thy pledged faith to meet me? soon

An hour beyond thy trothplight noon

Shall strike my death-bell, and thy boon

 Is this, that here I die.

'My curse for all thy gifts may be
Heavier than death or night on thee;
For now this sword thou gavest me
Shall set me from thy bondage free.'

 And there the man had died self-slain,
But Balen leapt on him and caught
The blind fierce hand that fain had wrought
Self-murder, stung with fire of thought,
 As rage makes anguish fain.

Then, mad for thwarted grief, 'Let go
My hand,' the fool of wrath and woe
Cried, 'or I slay thee.' Scarce the glow
In Balen's cheek and eye might show,
 As dawn shows day while seas lie chill,
He heard, though pity took not heed,
But smiled and spake, 'That shall not need:
What man may do to bid you speed
 I, so God speed me, will.'

And the other craved his name, beguiled
By hope that made his madness mild.
Again Sir Balen spake and smiled:
'My name is Balen, called the Wild
    By knights whom kings and courts make tame
Because I ride alone afar
And follow but my soul for star.'
'Ah, sir, I know the knight you are
    And all your fiery fame.

'The knight that bears two swords I know,
Most praised of all men, friend and foe,
For prowess of your hands, that show
Dark war the way where balefires glow
    And kindle glory like the dawn's.'
So spake the sorrowing knight, and stood
As one whose heart fresh hope made good:
And forth they rode by wold and wood
    And down the glimmering lawns.

And Balen craved his name who rode

Beside him, where the wild wood glowed

With joy to feel how noontide flowed

Through glade and glen and rough green road

    Till earth grew joyful as the sea.

'My name is Garnysshe of the Mount,

A poor man's son of none account,'

He said, 'where springs of loftier fount

    Laugh loud with pride to be.

'But strength in weakness lives and stands

As rocks that rise through shifting sands;

And for the prowess of my hands

One made me knight and gave me lands,

    Duke Hermel, lord from far to near,

Our prince; and she that loved me—she

I love, and deemed she loved but me,

His daughter, pledged her faith to be

    Ere now beside me here.'

And Balen, brief of speech as light
Whose word, beheld of depth and height,
Strikes silence through the stars of night,
Spake, and his face as dawn's grew bright,
    For hope to help a happier man,
' How far then lies she hence ? '   ' By this,'
Her lover sighed and said, ' I wis,
Not six fleet miles the passage is,
    And straight as thought could span.'

So rode they swift and sure, and found
A castle walled and dyked around :
And Balen, as a warrior bound
On search where hope might fear to sound
    The darkness of the deeps of doubt,
Made entrance through the guardless gate
As life, while hope in life grows great,
Makes way between the doors of fate
    That death may pass thereout.

Through many a glorious chamber, wrought
For all delight that love's own thought
Might dream or dwell in, Balen sought
And found of all he looked for nought,
    For like a shining shell her bed
Shone void and vacant of her : thence
Through devious wonders bright and dense
He passed and saw with shame-struck sense
    Where shame and faith lay dead.

Down in a sweet small garden, fair
With flowerful joy in the ardent air,
He saw, and raged with loathing, where
She lay with love-dishevelled hair
    Beneath a broad bright laurel tree
And clasped in amorous arms a knight,
The unloveliest that his scornful sight
Had dwelt on yet ; a shame the bright
    Broad noon might shrink to see.

And thence in wrathful hope he turned,
Hot as the heart within him burned,
To meet the knight whose love, so spurned
And spat on and made nought of, yearned
    And dreamed and hoped and lived in vain,
And said, 'I have found her sleeping fast,'
And led him where the shadows cast
From leaves wherethrough light winds ran past
    Screened her from sun and rain.

But Garnysshe, seeing, reeled as he stood
Like a tree, kingliest of the wood,
Half hewn through : and the burning blood
Through lips and nostrils burst aflood :
    And gathering back his rage and might
As broken breakers rally and roar
The loud wind down that drives off shore,
He smote their heads off : there no more
    Their life might shame the light.

Then turned he back toward Balen, mad
With grief, and said, 'The grief I had
Was nought: ere this my life was glad:
Thou hast done this deed: I was but sad
    And fearful how my hope might fare:
I had lived my sorrow down, hadst thou
Not shown me what I saw but now.'
The sorrow and scorn on Balen's brow
    Bade silence curb him there.

And Balen answered: 'What I did
I did to hearten thee and bid
Thy courage know that shame should rid
A man's high heart of love that hid
    Blind shame within its core: God knows,
I did, to set a bondman free,
But as I would thou hadst done by me,
That seeing what love must die to see
    Love's end might well be woe's.'

'Alas,' the woful weakling said,
'I have slain what most I loved: I have shed
The blood most near my heart: the head
Lies cold as earth, defiled and dead,
    That all my life was lighted by,
That all my soul bowed down before,
And now may bear with life no more :
For now my sorrow that I bore
    Is twofold, and I die.'

Then with his red wet sword he rove
His breast in sunder, where it clove
Life, and no pulse against it strove,
So sure and strong the deep stroke drove
    Deathward: and Balen, seeing him dead,
Rode thence, lest folk would say he had slain
Those three; and ere three days again
Had seen the sun's might wax and wane,
    Far forth he had spurred and sped.

And riding past a cross whereon
Broad golden letters written shone,
Saying, ' No knight born may ride alone
Forth toward this castle,' and all the stone
    Glowed in the sun's glare even as though
Blood stained it from the crucified
Dead burden of one that there had died,
An old hoar man he saw beside
    Whose face was wan as woe.

' Balen the Wild,' he said, ' this way
Thy way lies not : thou hast passed to-day
Thy bands : but turn again, and stay
Thy passage, while thy soul hath sway
    Within thee, and through God's good power
It will avail thee : ' and anon
His likeness as a cloud was gone,
And Balen's heart within him shone
    Clear as the cloudless hour.

Nor fate nor fear might overcast
The soul now near its peace at last.
Suddenly, thence as forth he past,
A mighty and a deadly blast
    Blown of a hunting-horn he heard,
As when the chase hath nobly sped.
' That blast is blown for me,' he said,
' The prize am I who am yet not dead,'
    And smiled upon the word.

As toward a royal hart's death rang
That note, whence all the loud wood sang
With winged and living sound that sprang
Like fire, and keen as fire's own fang
    Pierced the sweet silence that it slew.
But nought like death or strife was here :
Fair semblance and most goodly cheer
They made him, they whose troop drew near
    As death among them drew.

A hundred ladies well arrayed
And many a knight well weaponed made
That kindly show of cheer : the glade
Shone round them till its very shade
    Lightened and laughed from grove to lawn
To hear and see them : so they brought
Within a castle fair as thought
Could dream that wizard hands had wrought
    The guest among them drawn.

All manner of glorious joy was there :
Harping and dancing, loud and fair,
And minstrelsy that made of air
Fire, so like fire its raptures were.
    Then the chief lady spake on high :
' Knight with the two swords, one of two
Must help you here or fall from you :
For needs you now must have ado
    And joust with one hereby.

'A good knight guards an island here
Against all swords that chance brings near,
And there with stroke of sword and spear
Must all for whom these halls make cheer
    Fight, and redeem or yield up life.'
'An evil custom,' Balen said,
'Is this, that none whom chance hath led
Hither, if knighthood crown his head,
    May pass unstirred to strife.'

'You shall not have ado to fight
Here save against one only knight,'
She said, and all her face grew bright
As hell-fire, lit with hungry light
    That wicked laughter touched with flame.
'Well, since I shall thereto,' said he,
'I am ready at heart as death for me:
Fain would I be where death should be
    And life should lose its name.

'But travelling men whose goal afar
Shines as a cloud-constraining star
Are often weary, and wearier are
Their steeds that feel each fret and jar
  Wherewith the wild ways wound them: yet,
Albeit my horse be weary, still
My heart is nowise weary; will
Sustains it even till death fulfil
  My trust upon him set.'

'Sir,' said a knight thereby that stood,
'Meseems your shield is now not good
But worn with warrior work, nor could
Sustain in strife the strokes it would:
  A larger will I lend you.' 'Ay,
Thereof I thank you,' Balen said,
Being single of heart as one that read
No face aright whence faith had fled,
  Nor dreamed that faith could fly.

And so he took that shield unknown
And left for treason's touch his own,
And toward that island rode alone,
Nor heard the blast against him blown
 Sound in the wind's and water's sound,
But hearkening toward the stream's edge heard
Nought save the soft stream's rippling word,
Glad with the gladness of a bird,
 That sang to the air around.

And there against the water-side
He saw, fast moored to rock and ride,
A fair great boat anear abide
Like one that waits the turning tide,
 Wherein embarked his horse and he
Passed over toward no kindly strand:
And where they stood again on land
There stood a maiden hard at hand
 Who seeing them wept to see.

And ' O knight Balen,' was her cry,
' Why have ye left your own shield? why
Come hither out of time to die?
For had ye kept your shield, thereby
    Ye had yet been known, and died not here.
Great pity it is of you this day
As ever was of knight, or may
Be ever, seeing in war's bright way
    Praise knows not Balen's peer.'

And Balen said, ' Thou hast heard my name
Right : it repenteth me, though shame
May tax me not with base men's blame,
That ever, hap what will, I came
    Within this country ; yet, being come,
For shame I may not turn again
Now, that myself and nobler men
May scorn me : now is more than then,
    And faith bids fear be dumb.

'Be it life or death, my chance I take,
Be it life's to build or death's to break:
And fall what may, me lists not make
Moan for sad life's or death's sad sake.'
 Then looked he on his armour, glad
And high of heart, and found it strong:
And all his soul became a song
And soared in prayer that soared not long,
 For all the hope it had.

Then saw he whence against him came
A steed whose trappings shone like flame,
And he that rode him showed the same
Fierce colour, bright as fire or fame,
 But dark the visors were as night
That hid from Balen Balan's face,
And his from Balan: God's own grace
Forsook them for a shadowy space
 Where darkness cast out light.

The two swords girt that Balen bare
Gave Balan for a breath's while there
Pause, wondering if indeed it were
Balen his brother, bound to dare
    The chance of that unhappy quest :
But seeing not as he thought to see
His shield, he deemed it was not he,
And so, as fate bade sorrow be,
    They laid their spears in rest.

So mighty was the course they ran
With spear to spear so great of span,
Each fell back stricken, man by man,
Horse by horse, borne down : so the ban
    That wrought by doom against them wrought :
But Balen by his falling steed
Was bruised the sorer, being indeed
Way-weary, like a rain-bruised reed,
    With travel ere he fought.

And Balen rose again from swoon
First, and went toward him: all too soon
He too then rose, and the evil boon
Of strength came back, and the evil tune
 Of battle unnatural made again
Mad music as for death's wide ear
Listening and hungering toward the near
Last sigh that life or death might hear
 At last from dying men.

Balan smote Balen first, and clove
His lifted shield that rose and strove
In vain against the stroke that drove
Down: as the web that morning wove
 Of glimmering pearl from spray to spray
Dies when the strong sun strikes it, so
Shrank the steel, tempered thrice to show
Strength, as the mad might of the blow
 Shore Balen's helm away.

Then turning as a turning wave
Against the land-wind, blind and brave
In hope that dreams despair may save,
With even the unhappy sword that gave
    The gifts of fame and fate in one
He smote his brother, and there had nigh
Felled him: and while they breathed, his eye
Glanced up, and saw beneath the sky
    Sights fairer than the sun.

The towers of all the castle there
Stood full of ladies, blithe and fair
As the earth beneath and the amorous air
About them and above them were:
    So toward the blind and fateful fight
Again those brethren went, and sore
Were all the strokes they smote and bore,
And breathed again, and fell once more
    To battle in their sight.

With blood that either spilt and bled
Was all the ground they fought on red,
And each knight's hauberk hewn and shred
Left each unmailed and naked, shed
    From off them even as mantles cast:
And oft they breathed, and drew but breath
Brief as the word strong sorrow saith,
And poured and drank the draught of death,
    Till fate was full at last.

And Balan, younger born than he
Whom darkness bade him slay, and be
Slain, as in mist where none may see
If aught abide or fall or flee,
    Drew back a little and laid him down,
Dying: but Balen stood, and said,
As one between the quick and dead
Might stand and speak, 'What good knight's head
    Hath won this mortal crown?

'What knight art thou? for never I
Who now beside thee dead shall die
Found yet the knight afar or nigh
That matched me.'   Then his brother's eye
    Flashed pride and love; he spake and smiled
And felt in death life's quickening flame,
And answered: 'Balan is my name,
The good knight Balen's brother; fame
    Calls and miscalls him wild.'

The cry from Balen's lips that sprang
Sprang sharper than his sword's stroke rang.
More keen than death's or memory's fang,
Through sense and soul the shuddering pang
    Shivered: and scarce he had cried, 'Alas
That ever I should see this day,'
When sorrow swooned from him away
As blindly back he fell, and lay
    Where sleep lets anguish pass.

But Balan rose on hands and knees
And crawled by childlike dim degrees
Up toward his brother, as a breeze
Creeps wingless over sluggard seas
    When all the wind's heart fails it : so
Beneath their mother's eyes had he,
A babe that laughed with joy to be,
Made toward him standing by her knee
    For love's sake long ago.

Then, gathering strength up for a space,
From off his brother's dying face
With dying hands that wrought apace
While death and life would grant them grace
    He loosed his helm and knew not him,
So scored with blood it was, and hewn
Athwart with darkening wounds : but soon
Life strove and shuddered through the swoon
    Wherein its light lay dim.

And sorrow set these chained words free :
'O Balan, O my brother ! me
Thou hast slain, and I, my brother, thee :
And now far hence, on shore and sea,
    Shall all the wide world speak of us.'
'Alas,' said Balan, 'that I might
Not know you, seeing two swords were dight
About you ; now the unanswering sight
    Hath here found answer thus.

'Because you bore another shield
Than yours, that even ere youth could wield
Like arms with manhood's tried and steeled
Shone as my star of battle-field,
    I deemed it surely might not be
My brother.' Then his brother spake
Fiercely : 'Would God, for thy sole sake,
I had my life again, to take
    Revenge for only thee !

'For all this deadly work was wrought
Of one false knight's false word and thought,
Whose mortal craft and counsel caught
And snared my faith who doubted nought,
    And made me put my shield away.
Ah, might I live, I would destroy
That castle for its customs : joy
There makes of grief a deadly toy,
    And death makes night of day.'

'Well done were that, if aught were done
Well ever here beneath the sun,'
Said Balan : 'better work were none :
For hither since I came and won
    A woful honour born of death,
When here my hap it was to slay
A knight who kept this island way,
I might not pass by night or day
    Hence, as this token saith.

'No more shouldst thou, for all the might
Of heart and hand that seals thee knight
Most noble of all that see the light,
Brother, hadst thou but slain in fight
    Me, and arisen unscathed and whole,
As would to God thou hadst risen! though here
Light is as darkness, hope as fear,
And love as hate: and none draws near
    Save toward a mortal goal.'

Then, fair as any poison-flower
Whose blossom blights the withering bower
Whereon its blasting breath has power,
Forth fared the lady of the tower
    With many a lady and many a knight,
And came across the water-way
Even where on death's dim border lay
Those brethren sent of her to slay
    And die in kindless fight.

And all those hard light hearts were swayed
With pity passing like a shade
That stays not, and may be not stayed,
To hear the mutual moan they made,
    Each to behold his brother die,
Saying, ' Both we came out of one tomb,
One star-crossed mother's woful womb,
And so within one grave-pit's gloom
    Untimely shall we lie.'

And Balan prayed, as God should bless
That lady for her gentleness,
That where the battle's mortal stress
Had made for them perforce to press
    The bed whence never man may rise
They twain, free now from hopes and fears,
Might sleep ; and she, as one that hears,
Bowed her bright head : and very tears
    Fell from her cold fierce eyes.

THE TALE OF BALEN

Then Balen prayed her send a priest
To housel them, that ere they ceased
The hansel of the heavenly feast
That fills with light from the answering east
    The sunset of the life of man
Might bless them, and their lips be kissed
With death's requickening eucharist,
And death's and life's dim sunlit mist
    Pass as a stream that ran.

And so their dying rites were done:
And Balen, seeing the death-struck sun
Sink, spake as he whose goal is won:
'Now, when our trophied tomb is one,
    And over us our tale is writ,
How two that loved each other, two
Born and begotten brethren, slew
Each other, none that reads anew
    Shall choose but weep for it.

'And no good knight and no good man
Whose eye shall ever come to scan
The record of the imperious ban
That made our life so sad a span
    Shall read or hear, who shall not pray
For us for ever.' Then anon
Died Balan; but the sun was gone,
And deep the stars of midnight shone,
    Ere Balen passed away.

And there low lying, as hour on hour
Fled, all his life in all its flower
Came back as in a sunlit shower
Of dreams, when sweet-souled sleep has power
    On life less sweet and glad to be.
He drank the draught of life's first wine
Again: he saw the moorland shine,
The rioting rapids of the Tyne,
    The woods, the cliffs, the sea.

The joy that lives at heart and home,
The joy to rest, the joy to roam,
The joy of crags and scaurs he clomb,
The rapture of the encountering foam
    Embraced and breasted of the boy,
The first good steed his knees bestrode,
The first wild sound of songs that flowed
Through ears that thrilled and heart that glowed,
    Fulfilled his death with joy.

So, dying not as a coward that dies
And dares not look in death's dim eyes
Straight as the stars on seas and skies
Whence moon and sun recoil and rise,
    He looked on life and death, and slept.
And there with morning Merlin came,
And on the tomb that told their fame
He wrote by Balan's Balen's name,
    And gazed thereon, and wept.

For all his heart within him yearned
With pity like as fire that burned.
The fate his fateful eye discerned
Far off now dimmed it, ere he turned
    His face toward Camelot, to tell
Arthur of all the storms that woke
Round Balen, and the dolorous stroke,
And how that last blind battle broke
    The consummated spell.

'Alas,' King Arthur said, 'this day
I have heard the worst that woe might say:
For in this world that wanes away
I know not two such knights as they.'
    This is the tale that memory writes
Of men whose names like stars shall stand,
Balen and Balan, sure of hand,
Two brethren of Northumberland,
    In life and death good knights.

MR. SWINBURNE'S WORKS.

SELECTIONS FROM THE POETICAL WORKS OF A. C. SWINBURNE. Fcp. 8vo. 6s.
ATALANTA IN CALYDON. Crown 8vo. 6s.
CHASTELARD: a Tragedy. Crown 8vo. 7s.
POEMS AND BALLADS. First Series. Crown 8vo. or fcp. 8vo. 9s.
POEMS AND BALLADS. Second Series. Crown 8vo. 9s.
POEMS AND BALLADS. Third Series. Crown 8vo. 7s.
SONGS BEFORE SUNRISE. Crown 8vo. 10s. 6d.
BOTHWELL: a Tragedy. Crown 8vo. 12s. 6d.
SONGS OF TWO NATIONS. Crown 8vo. 6s.
GEORGE CHAPMAN. (See Vol. II. of G. Chapman's Works.) Crown 8vo. 6s.
ESSAYS AND STUDIES. Crown 8vo. 12s.
ERECHTHEUS: a Tragedy. Crown 8vo. 6s.
A NOTE ON CHARLOTTE BRONTË. Crown 8vo. 6s.
A STUDY OF SHAKESPEARE. Crown 8vo. 8s.
SONGS OF THE SPRINGTIDES. Crown 8vo. 6s.
STUDIES IN SONG. Crown 8vo. 7s.
MARY STUART: a Tragedy. Crown 8vo. 8s.
TRISTRAM OF LYONESSE. Crown 8vo. 9s.
A CENTURY OF ROUNDELS. Small 4to. 8s.
A MIDSUMMER HOLIDAY. Crown 8vo. 7s.
MARINO FALIERO: a Tragedy. Crown 8vo. 6s.
A STUDY OF VICTOR HUGO. Crown 8vo. 6s.
MISCELLANIES. Crown 8vo. 12s.
LOCRINE: a Tragedy. Crown 8vo. 6s.
A STUDY OF BEN JONSON. Crown 8vo. 7s.
THE SISTERS: a Tragedy. Crown 8vo. 6s.
ASTROPHEL, &c. Crown 8vo. 7s.
STUDIES IN PROSE AND POETRY. Crown 8vo. 9s.

London: CHATTO & WINDUS, 214 Piccadilly.

[*March* 1896.

LIST OF BOOKS PUBLISHED BY

CHATTO & WINDUS
214 PICCADILLY, LONDON, W.

About (Edmond).—The Fellah: An Egyptian Novel. Translated by Sir RANDAL ROBERTS. Post 8vo, illustrated boards, 2s.

Adams (W. Davenport), Works by.
A **Dictionary of the Drama**: being a comprehensive Guide to the Plays, Playwrights, Players, and Playhouses of the United Kingdom and America, from the Earliest Times to the Present Day. Crown 8vo, half-bound, 12s. 6d. [*Preparing.*
Quips and Quiddities. Selected by W. DAVENPORT ADAMS. Post 8vo, cloth limp, 2s. 6d.

Agony Column (The) of 'The Times,' from 1800 to 1870. Edited, with an Introduction, by ALICE CLAY. Post 8vo, cloth limp, 2s. 6d.

Aidé (Hamilton), Novels by. Post 8vo, illustrated boards, 2s. each.
Carr of Carrlyon. | **Confidences.**

Albert (Mary).—Brooke Finchley's Daughter. Post 8vo, picture boards, 2s.; cloth limp, 2s. 6d.

Alden (W. L.).—A Lost Soul: Being the Confession and Defence of Charles Lindsay. Fcap. 8vo, cloth boards, 1s. 6d.

Alexander (Mrs.), Novels by. Post 8vo, illustrated boards, 2s. each.
Maid, Wife, or Widow? | **Valerie's Fate.**

Allen (F. M.).—Green as Grass. With a Frontispiece. Crown 8vo, cloth, 3s. 6d.

Allen (Grant), Works by.
The Evolutionist at Large. Crown 8vo, cloth extra, 6s.
Post-Prandial Philosophy. Crown 8vo, art linen, 3s. 6d.
Moorland Idylls. Crown 8vo, cloth decorated, 6s.

Crown 8vo, cloth extra, 3s. 6d. each; post 8vo, illustrated boards, 2s. each.

Philistia.	In all Shades.	Dumaresq's Daughter.
Babylon. 12 Illustrations.	The Devil's Die.	The Duchess of Powysland.
Strange Stories. Frontis.	This Mortal Coil.	Blood Royal.
The Beckoning Hand.	The Tents of Shem. Frontis.	Ivan Greet's Masterpiece.
For Maimie's Sake.	The Great Taboo.	The Scallywag. 24 Illusts.

Crown 8vo, cloth extra, 3s. 6d. each.
At Market Value. | **Under Sealed Orders.**

Dr. Palliser's Patient. Fcap. 8vo, cloth boards, 1s. 6d.

Anderson (Mary).—Othello's Occupation: A Novel. Crown 8vo, cloth, 3s. 6d.

Arnold (Edwin Lester), Stories by.
The Wonderful Adventures of Phra the Phœnician. Crown 8vo, cloth extra, with 12 Illustrations by H. M. PAGET, 3s. 6d.; post 8vo, illustrated boards, 2s.
The Constable of St. Nicholas. With Frontispiece by S. L. WOOD. Crown 8vo, cloth, 3s. 6d.

Artemus Ward's Works. With Portrait and Facsimile. Crown 8vo, cloth extra, 7s. 6d.—Also a POPULAR EDITION, post 8vo, picture boards, 2s.
The Genial Showman: The Life and Adventures of ARTEMUS WARD. By EDWARD P. HINGSTON. With a Frontispiece. Crown 8vo, cloth extra, 3s. 6d.

Ashton (John), Works by. Crown 8vo, cloth extra, 7s. 6d. each.
History of the Chap-Books of the 18th Century. With 334 Illustrations.
Social Life in the Reign of Queen Anne. With 85 Illustrations.
Humour, Wit, and Satire of the Seventeenth Century. With 82 Illustrations.
English Caricature and Satire on Napoleon the First. With 115 Illustrations.
Modern Street Ballads. With 57 Illustrations.

Bacteria, Yeast Fungi, and Allied Species, A Synopsis of. By W. B. GROVE, B.A. With 87 Illustrations. Crown 8vo, cloth extra, 3s. 6d.

Bardsley (Rev. C. Wareing, M.A.), Works by.
English Surnames: Their Sources and Significations. Crown 8vo, cloth, 7s. 6d.
Curiosities of Puritan Nomenclature. Crown 8vo, cloth extra, 6s.

Baring Gould (Sabine, Author of 'John Herring,' &c.), Novels by. Crown 8vo, cloth extra, 3s. 6d. each; post 8vo, illustrated boards, 2s. each.
Red Spider. | Eve.

Barr (Robert: Luke Sharp), Stories by. Cr. 8vo, cl., 3s. 6d. each.
In a Steamer Chair. With Frontispiece and Vignette by DEMAIN HAMMOND.
From Whose Bourne, &c, With 47 Illustrations by HAL HURST and others.
A Woman Intervenes. With 8 Illustrations by HAL HURST. Crown 8vo, cloth extra, 6s.
Revenge! With numerous Illustrations. Crown 8vo, cloth extra, 6s. [*Shortly*.

Barrett (Frank), Novels by.
Post 8vo, illustrated boards, 2s. each; cloth, 2s. 6d. each.
Fettered for Life. | A Prodigal's Progress.
The Sin of Olga Zassoulich. | John Ford; and His Helpmate.
Between Life and Death. | A Recoiling Vengeance.
Folly Morrison. | Honest Davie. | Lieut. Barnabas. | Found Guilty.
Little Lady Linton. | For Love and Honour.
The Woman of the Iron Bracelets. Cr. 8vo, cloth, 3s. 6d.; post 8vo, boards, 2s.; cl. limp, 2s. 6d.
The Harding Scandal. 2 vols., 10s. net. [*Shortly*.

Barrett (Joan).—Monte Carlo Stories. Fcap. 8vo, cloth, 1s. 6d.

Beaconsfield, Lord. By T. P. O'CONNOR, M.P. Cr. 8vo, cloth, 5s.

Beauchamp (Shelsley).—Grantley Grange. Post 8vo, boards, 2s.

Beautiful Pictures by British Artists: A Gathering of Favourites from the Picture Galleries, engraved on Steel. Imperial 4to, cloth extra, gilt edges, 21s.

Besant (Sir Walter) and James Rice, Novels by.
Crown 8vo, cloth extra, 3s. 6d. each; post 8vo, illustrated boards, 2s. each; cloth limp, 2s. 6d. each.
Ready-Money Mortiboy. | By Celia's Arbour.
My Little Girl. | The Chaplain of the Fleet.
With Harp and Crown. | The Seamy Side.
This Son of Vulcan. | The Case of Mr. Lucraft, &c.
The Golden Butterfly. | 'Twas in Trafalgar's Bay, &c.
The Monks of Thelema. | The Ten Years' Tenant, &c.
*** There is also a LIBRARY EDITION of the above Twelve Volumes, handsomely set in new type on a large crown 8vo page, and bound in cloth extra, 6s. each; and a POPULAR EDITION of The Golden Butterfly, medium 8vo. 6d.; cloth, 1s.—NEW EDITIONS, printed in large type on crown 8vo laid paper, bound in figured cloth, 3s. 6d. each, are also in course of publication.

Besant (Sir Walter), Novels by.
Crown 8vo, cloth extra, 3s. 6d. each; post 8vo, illustrated boards, 2s. each; cloth limp, 2s. 6d. each.
All Sorts and Conditions of Men. With 12 Illustrations by FRED. BARNARD
The Captains' Room, &c. With Frontispiece by E. J. WHEELER.
All in a Garden Fair. With 6 Illustrations by HARRY FURNISS.
Dorothy Forster. With Frontispiece by CHARLES GREEN.
Uncle Jack, and other Stories. | Children of Gibeon.
The World Went Very Well Then. With 12 Illustrations by A. FORESTIER.
Herr Paulus: His Rise, his Greatness, and his Fall. | The Bell of St. Paul's.
For Faith and Freedom. With Illustrations by A. FORESTIER and F. WADDY.
To Call Her Mine, &c. With 9 Illustrations by A. FORESTIER.
The Holy Rose, &c. With Frontispiece by F. BARNARD.
Armorel of Lyonesse: A Romance of To-day. With 12 Illustrations by F. BARNARD.
St. Katherine's by the Tower. With 12 Illustrations by C. GREEN.
Verbena Camellia Stephanotis, &c. With a Frontispiece by GORDON BROWNE.
The Ivory Gate. | The Rebel Queen.

Beyond the Dreams of Avarice. With 12 Illusts. by W. H. HYDE. Crown 8vo, cloth extra, 3s. 6d.
In Deacon's Orders, &c. With Frontispiece by A. FORESTIER. Crown 8vo, cloth, 6s.
The Master Craftsman. 2 vols., crown 8vo, 10s. net. [*May*.
Fifty Years Ago. With 144 Plates and Woodcuts. Crown 8vo, cloth extra, 5s.
The Eulogy of Richard Jefferies. With Portrait. Crown 8vo, cloth extra, 6s.
London. With 125 Illustrations. Demy 8vo, cloth extra, 7s. 6d.
Westminster. With Etched Frontispiece by F. S. WALKER, R.P.E., and 130 Illustrations by WILLIAM PATTEN and others. Demy 8vo, cloth, 18s.
Sir Richard Whittington. With Frontispiece. Crown 8vo, art linen, 3s. 6d.
Gaspard de Coligny. With a Portrait. Crown 8vo, art linen, 3s. 6d.
As we Are; As we May Be: Social Essays. Crown 8vo, linen, 6s. [*Shortly*.

Bechstein (Ludwig).—As Pretty as Seven, and other German Stories. With Additional Tales by the Brothers GRIMM, and 98 Illustrations by RICHTER. Square 8vo, cloth extra, 6s. 6d.; gilt edges, 7s. 6d.

Beerbohm (Julius).—Wanderings in Patagonia; or, Life among the Ostrich-Hunters. With Illustrations. Crown 8vo, cloth extra, 3s. 6d.

Bellew (Frank).—The Art of Amusing: A Collection of Graceful Arts, Games, Tricks, Puzzles, and Charades. With 300 Illustrations. Crown 8vo, cloth extra, 4s. 6d.

Bennett (W. C., LL.D.).—Songs for Sailors. Post 8vo, cl. limp, 2s.

Bewick (Thomas) and his Pupils. By AUSTIN DOBSON. With 95 Illustrations. Square 8vo, cloth extra, 6s.

Bierce (Ambrose).—In the Midst of Life: Tales of Soldiers and Civilians. Crown 8vo, cloth extra, 6s.; post 8vo, illustrated boards, 2s.

Bill Nye's History of the United States. With 146 Illustrations by F. OPPER. Crown 8vo, cloth extra, 3s. 6d.

Bire (Edmond). — Diary of a Citizen of Paris during 'The Terror.' Translated and Edited by JOHN DE VILLIERS. With 2 Photogravures. Two Vols., 8vo, cloth, 21s. [*Shortly.*

Blackburn's (Henry) Art Handbooks.
Academy Notes, 1875, 1877-86, 1889, 1890, 1892-1895, Illustrated, each 1s.
Academy Notes, 1896. 1s. [*May.*
Academy Notes, 1875-79. Complete in One Vol., with 600 Illustrations. Cloth, 6s.
Academy Notes, 1880-84. Complete in One Vol., with 700 Illustrations. Cloth, 6s.
Academy Notes, 1890-94. Complete in One Vol., with 800 Illustrations. Cloth, 7s. 6d.
Grosvenor Notes, 1877. 6d.
Grosvenor Notes, separate years from 1878-1890, each 1s.
Grosvenor Notes, Vol. I., 1877-82. With 300 Illustrations. Demy 8vo, cloth, 6s.
The Paris Salon, 1895. With 300 Facsimile Sketches. 3s.
Grosvenor Notes, Vol. II., 1883-87. With 300 Illustrations. Demy 8vo, cloth, 6s.
Grosvenor Notes, Vol. III., 1888-90. With 230 Illustrations. Demy 8vo, cloth, 3s. 6d.
The New Gallery, 1888-1895. With numerous Illustrations, each 1s.
The New Gallery, 1896. [*May.*
The New Gallery, Vol. I., 1888-1892. With 250 Illustrations. Demy 8vo, cloth, 6s.
English Pictures at the National Gallery. With 114 Illustrations. 1s.
Old Masters at the National Gallery. With 128 Illustrations. 1s. 6d.
Illustrated Catalogue to the National Gallery. With 242 Illusts. Demy 8vo, cloth, 3s.

Blind (Mathilde), Poems by.
The Ascent of Man. Crown 8vo, cloth, 5s.
Dramas in Miniature. With a Frontispiece by F. MADOX BROWN. Crown 8vo, cloth, 5s.
Songs and Sonnets. Fcap. 8vo, vellum and gold, 5s.
Birds of Passage: Songs of the Orient and Occident. Second Edition. Crown 8vo, linen, 6s. net.

Bourget (Paul).—A Living Lie. Translated by JOHN DE VILLIERS. With special Preface for the English Edition. Crown 8vo, cloth, 3s. 6d.

Bourne (H. R. Fox), Books by.
English Merchants: Memoirs in Illustration of the Progress of British Commerce. With numerous Illustrations. Crown 8vo, cloth extra, 7s. 6d.
English Newspapers: Chapters in the History of Journalism. Two Vols., demy 8vo, cloth, 25s.
The Other Side of the Emin Pasha Relief Expedition. Crown 8vo, cloth, 6s.

Bowers (George).—Leaves from a Hunting Journal. Coloured Plates. Oblong folio, half-bound, 21s.

Boyle (Frederick), Works by. Post 8vo, illustrated bds., 2s. each.
Chronicles of No-Man's Land. | Camp Notes. | Savage Life.

Brand (John).—Observations on Popular Antiquities; chiefly illustrating the Origin of our Vulgar Customs, Ceremonies, and Superstitions. With the Additions of Sir HENRY ELLIS, and numerous Illustrations. Crown 8vo, cloth extra, 7s. 6d.

Brewer (Rev. Dr.), Works by.
The Reader's Handbook of Allusions, References, Plots, and Stories. Seventeenth Thousand. Crown 8vo, cloth extra, 7s. 6d.
Authors and their Works, with the Dates: Being the Appendices to 'The Reader's Handbook,' separately printed. Crown 8vo, cloth limp, 2s.
A Dictionary of Miracles. Crown 8vo, cloth extra, 7s. 6d.

Brewster (Sir David), Works by. Post 8vo, cloth, 4s. 6d. each.
More Worlds than One: Creed of the Philosopher and Hope of the Christian. With Plates.
The Martyrs of Science: GALILEO, TYCHO BRAHE, and KEPLER. With Portraits.
Letters on Natural Magic. With numerous Illustrations.

Brillat-Savarin.— Gastronomy as a Fine Art. Translated by R. E. ANDERSON, M.A. Post 8vo, half-bound, 2s.

Brydges (Harold).—Uncle Sam at Home. With 91 Illustrations. Post 8vo, illustrated boards, 2s.; cloth limp, 2s. 6d.

Buchanan (Robert), Novels, &c., by.
Crown 8vo, cloth extra, 3s. 6d. each; pos 8vo, illustrated boards, 2s. each.

The Shadow of the Sword.
A Child of Nature. With Frontispiece.
God and the Man. With 11 Illustrations by FRED. BARNARD.
The Martyrdom of Madeline. With Frontispiece by A. W. COOPER.

Love Me for Ever. With Frontispiece.
Annan Water. | Foxglove Manor.
The New Abelard.
Matt: A Story of a Caravan. With Frontispiece.
The Master of the Mine. With Frontispiece.
The Heir of Linne. | Woman and the Man.

Crown 8vo, cloth extra, 3s. 6d. each.
Red and White Heather. | Rachel Dene.
Lady Kilpatrick. Crown 8vo, cloth extra, 6s.
The Wandering Jew: a Christmas Carol. Crown 8vo, cloth, 6s.

The Charlatan. By ROBERT BUCHANAN and HENRY MURRAY. With a Frontispiece by T. H. ROBINSON. Crown 8vo, cloth, 3s. 6d.

Burton (Richard F.).—The Book of the Sword. With over 400 Illustrations. Demy 4to, cloth extra, 32s.

Burton (Robert).—The Anatomy of Melancholy. With Translations of the Quotations. Demy 8vo, cloth extra, 7s. 6d.
Melancholy Anatomised: An Abridgment of BURTON'S ANATOMY. Post 8vo, half-bd., 2s. 6d.

Caine (T. Hall), Novels by. Crown 8vo, cloth extra, 3s. 6d. each..; post 8vo, illustrated boards, 2s. each; cloth limp, 2s. 6d. each.
The Shadow of a Crime. | A Son of Hagar. | The Deemster.
A LIBRARY EDITION of The Deemster is now ready; and one of The Shadow of a Crime is in preparation, set in new type, crown 8vo, cloth decorated, 6s. each.

Cameron (Commander V. Lovett).—The Cruise of the 'Black Prince' Privateer. Post 8vo, picture boards, 2s.

Cameron (Mrs. H. Lovett), Novels by. Post 8vo, illust. bds. 2s. ea.
Juliet's Guardian. | Deceivers Ever.

Carlyle (Jane Welsh), Life of. By Mrs. ALEXANDER IRELAND. With Portrait and Facsimile Letter. Small demy 8vo, cloth extra, 7s. 6d.

Carlyle (Thomas).—On the Choice of Books. Post 8vo, cl., 1s. 6d.
Correspondence of Thomas Carlyle and R. W. Emerson, 1834-1872. Edited by C. E. NORTON. With Portraits. Two Vols., crown 8vo, cloth, 24s.

Carruth (Hayden).—The Adventures of Jones. With 17 Illustrations. Fcap. 8vo, cloth, 2s.

Chambers (Robert W.), Stories of Paris Life by. Long fcap. 8vo, cloth, 2s. 6d. each.
The King in Yellow. | In the Quarter.

Chapman's (George), Works. Vol. I., Plays Complete, including the Doubtful Ones.—Vol. II., Poems and Minor Translations, with Essay by A. C. SWINBURNE.—Vol. III., Translations of the Iliad and Odyssey. Three Vols., crown 8vo, cloth, 6s. each.

Chapple (J. Mitchell).—The Minor Chord: The Story of a Prima Donna. Crown 8vo, cloth, 3s. 6d.

Chatto (W. A.) and J. Jackson.—A Treatise on Wood Engraving, Historical and Practical. With Chapter by H. G. BOHN, and 450 fine Illusts. Large 4to, half-leather, 28s.

Chaucer for Children: A Golden Key. By Mrs. H. R. HAWEIS. With 8 Coloured Plates and 30 Woodcuts. Crown 4to, cloth extra, 3s. 6d.
Chaucer for Schools. By Mrs. H. R. HAWEIS. Demy 8vo, cloth limp, 2s. 6d.

Chess, The Laws and Practice of. With an Analysis of the Openings. By HOWARD STAUNTON. Edited by R. B. WORMALD. Crown 8vo, cloth, 5s.
The Minor Tactics of Chess: A Treatise on the Deployment of the Forces in obedience to Strategic Principle. By F. K. YOUNG and E. C. HOWELL. Long fcap. 8vo, cloth, 2s. 6d.
The Hastings Chess Tournament Book (Aug.-Sept., 1895). Containing the Official Report of the 231 Games played in the Tournament, with Notes by the Players, and Diagrams of Interesting Positions; Portraits and Biographical Sketches of the Chess Masters; and an Account of the Congress and its surroundings. Crown 8vo, cloth extra, 7s. 6d. net. [Shortly.

Clare (Austin).—For the Love of a Lass. Post 8vo, 2s.; cl., 2s. 6d.

Clive (Mrs. Archer), Novels by. Post 8vo, illust. boards, 2s. each.
Paul Ferroll. | Why Paul Ferroll Killed his Wife.

Clodd (Edward, F.R.A.S.).—Myths and Dreams. Cr. 8vo, 3s. 6d.

Cobban (J. Maclaren), Novels by.
The Cure of Souls. Post 8vo, Illustrated boards, 2s.
The Red Sultan. Crown 8vo, cloth extra, 3s. 6d. ; post 8vo, illustrated boards, 2s.
The Burden of Isabel. Crown 8vo, cloth extra, 3s. 6d.

Coleman (John).—Players and Playwrights I have Known. Two Vols., demy 8vo, cloth, 24s.

Coleridge (M. E.).—The Seven Sleepers of Ephesus. Cloth, 1s. 6d.

Collins (C. Allston).—The Bar Sinister. Post 8vo, boards, 2s.

Collins (John Churton, M.A.), Books by.
Illustrations of Tennyson. Crown 8vo, cloth extra, 6s.
Jonathan Swift: A Biographical and Critical Study. Crown 8vo, cloth extra, 8s.

Collins (Mortimer and Frances), Novels by.
Crown 8vo, cloth extra, 3s. 6d. each ; post 8vo, illustrated boards, 2s. each.
From Midnight to Midnight. | Blacksmith and Scholar.
Transmigration. | You Play me False. | A Village Comedy.

Post 8vo, illustrated boards, 2s. each.
Sweet Anne Page. | A Fight with Fortune. | Sweet and Twenty. | Frances.

Collins (Wilkie), Novels by.
Crown 8vo, cloth extra, 3s. 6d. each ; post 8vo, illustrated boards, 2s. each ; cloth limp, 2s. 6d. each.
Antonina. With a Frontispiece by Sir JOHN GILBERT, R.A.
Basil. Illustrated by Sir JOHN GILBERT, R.A., and J. MAHONEY.
Hide and Seek. Illustrated by Sir JOHN GILBERT, R.A., and J. MAHONEY.
After Dark. With Illustrations by A. B. HOUGHTON. | The Two Destinies.
The Dead Secret. With a Frontispiece by Sir JOHN GILBERT, R.A.
Queen of Hearts. With a Frontispiece by Sir JOHN GILBERT, R.A.
The Woman in White. With Illustrations by Sir JOHN GILBERT, R.A., and F. A. FRASER.
No Name. With Illustrations by Sir J. E. MILLAIS, R.A., and A. W. COOPER.
My Miscellanies. With a Steel-plate Portrait of WILKIE COLLINS.
Armadale. With Illustrations by G. H. THOMAS.
The Moonstone. With Illustrations by G. DU MAURIER and F. A. FRASER.
Man and Wife. With Illustrations by WILLIAM SMALL.
Poor Miss Finch. Illustrated by G. DU MAURIER and EDWARD HUGHES.
Miss or Mrs.? With Illustrations by S. L. FILDES, R.A., and HENRY WOODS, A.R.A.
The New Magdalen. Illustrated by G. DU MAURIER and C. S. REINHARDT.
The Frozen Deep. Illustrated by G. DU MAURIER and J. MAHONEY.
The Law and the Lady. With Illustrations by S. L. FILDES, R.A., and SYDNEY HALL.
The Haunted Hotel. With Illustrations by ARTHUR HOPKINS.
The Fallen Leaves. | Heart and Science. | The Evil Genius.
Jezebel's Daughter. | 'I Say No.' | Little Novels. Frontis.
The Black Robe. | A Rogue's Life. | The Legacy of Cain.
Blind Love. With a Preface by Sir WALTER BESANT, and Illustrations by A. FORESTIER.

POPULAR EDITIONS. Medium 8vo, 6d. each ; cloth, 1s. each.
The Woman in White. | The Moonstone.

The Woman in White and The Moonstone in One Volume, medium 8vo, cloth, 2s.

Colman's (George) Humorous Works: 'Broad Grins,' 'My Nightgown and Slippers,' &c. With Life and Frontispiece. Crown 8vo, cloth extra, 7s. 6d.

Colquhoun (M. J.).—Every Inch a Soldier. Post 8vo, boards, 2s.

Colt-breaking, Hints on. By W. M. HUTCHISON. Cr. 8vo, cl., 3s. 6d.

Convalescent Cookery. By CATHERINE RYAN. Cr. 8vo, 1s.; cl., 1s. 6d.

Conway (Moncure D.), Works by.
Demonology and Devil-Lore. With 65 Illustrations. Two Vols., demy 8vo, cloth, 28s.
George Washington's Rules of Civility. Fcap. 8vo, Japanese vellum, 2s. 6d.

Cook (Dutton), Novels by.
Paul Foster's Daughter. Crown 8vo, cloth extra, 3s. 6d. ; post 8vo, illustrated boards, 2s.
Leo. Post 8vo, illustrated boards, 2s.

Cooper (Edward H.).—Geoffory Hamilton. Cr. 8vo, cloth, 3s. 6d.

Cornwall.—Popular Romances of the West of England; or, The Drolls, Traditions, and Superstitions of Old Cornwall. Collected by ROBERT HUNT, F.R.S. With two Steel Plates by GEORGE CRUIKSHANK. Crown 8vo, cloth, 7s. 6d.

Cotes (V. Cecil).—Two Girls on a Barge. With 44 Illustrations by F. H. TOWNSEND. Post 8vo, cloth, 2s. 6d.

Craddock (C. Egbert), Stories by.
The Prophet of the Great Smoky Mountains. Post 8vo, illustrated boards, 2s.
His Vanished Star. Crown 8vo, cloth extra, 3s. 6d.

Cram (Ralph Adams).—Black Spirits and White. Fcap. 8vo, cloth 1s. 6d.

Crellin (H. N.), Books by.
Romances of the Old Seraglio. With 28 Illustrations by S. L. WOOD. Crown 8vo, cloth, 3s. 6d.
Tales of the Caliph. Crown 8vo, cloth, 2s.
The Nazarenes: A Drama. Crown 8vo, 1s.

Crim (Matt.).—Adventures of a Fair Rebel. Crown 8vo, cloth extra, with a Frontispiece by DAN. BEARD, 3s. 6d.; post 8vo, illustrated boards, 2s.

Crockett (S. R.) and others.—Tales of Our Coast. By S. R. CROCKETT, GILBERT PARKER, HAROLD FREDERIC, 'Q.,' and W. CLARK RUSSELL. With 12 Illustrations by FRANK BRANGWYN. Crown 8vo, cloth, 3s. 6d. [*Shortly.*

Croker (Mrs. B. M.), Novels by. Crown 8vo, cloth extra, 3s. 6d. each; post 8vo, illustrated boards, 2s. each; cloth limp, 2s. 6d. each.
Pretty Miss Neville. | Diana Barrington. | A Family Likeness.
A Bird of Passage. | Proper Pride. | 'To Let.'
Village Tales and Jungle Tragedies.
Crown 8vo, cloth extra, 3s. 6d. each.
Mr. Jervis. | The Real Lady Hilda.
Married or Single? Three Vols., crown 8vo, 15s. net.

Cruikshank's Comic Almanack. Complete in TWO SERIES: The FIRST, from 1835 to 1843; the SECOND, from 1844 to 1853. A Gathering of the Best Humour of THACKERAY, HOOD, MAYHEW, ALBERT SMITH, A'BECKETT, ROBERT BROUGH, &c. With numerous Steel Engravings and Woodcuts by GEORGE CRUIKSHANK, HINE, LANDELLS, &c. Two Vols., crown 8vo, cloth gilt, 7s. 6d. each.
The Life of George Cruikshank. By BLANCHARD JERROLD. With 84 Illustrations and a Bibliography. Crown 8vo, cloth extra, 6s.

Cumming (C. F. Gordon), Works by. Demy 8vo, cl. ex., 8s. 6d. ea.
In the Hebrides. With an Autotype Frontispiece and 23 Illustrations.
In the Himalayas and on the Indian Plains. With 42 Illustrations.
Two Happy Years in Ceylon. With 28 Illustrations.
Via Cornwall to Egypt. With a Photogravure Frontispiece. Demy 8vo, cloth, 7s. 6d.

Cussans (John E.).—A Handbook of Heraldry; with Instructions for Tracing Pedigrees and Deciphering Ancient MSS., &c. Fourth Edition, revised, with 408 Woodcuts and 2 Coloured Plates. Crown 8vo, cloth extra, 6s.

Cyples (W.).—Hearts of Gold. Cr. 8vo, cl., 3s. 6d.; post 8vo, bds., 2s.

Daniel (George).—Merrie England in the Olden Time. With Illustrations by ROBERT CRUIKSHANK. Crown 8vo, cloth extra, 3s. 6d.

Daudet (Alphonse).—The Evangelist; or, Port Salvation. Crown 8vo, cloth extra, 3s. 6d.; post 8vo, illustrated boards, 2s.

Davenant (Francis, M.A.).—Hints for Parents on the Choice of a Profession for their Sons when Starting in Life. Crown 8vo, 1s.: cloth, 1s. 6d.

Davidson (Hugh Coleman).—Mr. Sadler's Daughters. With a Frontispiece by STANLEY WOOD. Crown 8vo, cloth extra, 3s. 6d.

Davies (Dr. N. E. Yorke-), Works by. Cr. 8vo, 1s. ea.; cl., 1s. 6d. ea.
One Thousand Medical Maxims and Surgical Hints.
Nursery Hints: A Mother's Guide in Health and Disease.
Foods for the Fat: A Treatise on Corpulency, and a Dietary for its Cure.
Aids to Long Life. Crown 8vo, 2s.; cloth limp, 2s. 6d.

Davies' (Sir John) Complete Poetical Works. Collected and Edited, with Introduction and Notes, by Rev. A. B. GROSART, D.D. Two Vols., crown 8vo, cloth, 12s.

Dawson (Erasmus, M.B.).—The Fountain of Youth. Crown 8vo, cloth extra, with Two Illustrations by HUME NISBET, 3s. 6d.; post 8vo, illustrated boards, 2s.

De Guerin (Maurice), The Journal of. Edited by G. S. TREBUTIEN. With a Memoir by SAINTE-BEUVE. Translated from the 20th French Edition by JESSIE P. FROTHINGHAM. Fcap. 8vo, half-bound, 2s. 6d.

De Maistre (Xavier).—A Journey Round my Room. Translated by Sir HENRY ATTWELL. Post 8vo, cloth limp, 2s. 6d.

De Mille (James).—A Castle in Spain. Crown 8vo, cloth extra, with a Frontispiece, 3s. 6d.; post 8vo, illustrated boards, 2s.

Derby (The): The Blue Ribbon of the Turf. With Brief Accounts of THE OAKS. By LOUIS HENRY CURZON. Crown 8vo, cloth limp, 2s. 6d.

Derwent (Leith), Novels by. Cr. 8vo, cl., 3s. 6d. ea.; post 8vo, 2s. ea.
Our Lady of Tears. | Circe's Lovers.

Dewar (T. R.).—A Ramble Round the Globe. With 220 Illustrations. Crown 8vo, cloth extra, 7s. 6d.

Dickens (Charles), Novels by. Post 8vo, illustrated boards, 2s. each.
Sketches by Boz. | Nicholas Nickleby. | Oliver Twist.

About England with Dickens. By ALFRED RIMMER. With 57 Illustrations by C. A. VANDERHOOF, ALFRED RIMMER, and others. Square 8vo, cloth extra, 7s. 6d.

Dictionaries.
A Dictionary of Miracles: Imitative, Realistic, and Dogmatic. By the Rev. E. C. BREWER, L.L.D. Crown 8vo, cloth extra, 7s. 6d.
The Reader's Handbook of Allusions, References, Plots, and Stories. By the Rev. E. C. BREWER, LL.D. With an ENGLISH BIBLIOGRAPHY. Crown 8vo, cloth extra, 7s. 6d.
Authors and their Works, with the Dates. Crown 8vo, cloth limp, 2s.
Familiar Short Sayings of Great Men. With Historical and Explanatory Notes by SAMUEL A. BENT, A.M. Crown 8vo, cloth extra, 7s. 6d.
The Slang Dictionary: Etymological, Historical, and Anecdotal. Crown 8vo, cloth, 6s. 6d.
Words, Facts, and Phrases: A Dictionary of Curious, Quaint, and Out-of-the-Way Matters. By ELIEZER EDWARDS. Crown 8vo, cloth extra, 7s. 6d.

Diderot.—The Paradox of Acting. Translated, with Notes, by WALTER HERRIES POLLOCK. With Preface by Sir HENRY IRVING. Crown 8vo, parchment, 4s. 6d.

Dobson (Austin), Works by.
Thomas Bewick and his Pupils. With 95 Illustrations. Square 8vo, cloth, 6s.
Four Frenchwomen. With Four Portraits. Crown 8vo, buckram, gilt top, 6s.
Eighteenth Century Vignettes. TWO SERIES Crown 8vo, buckram, 6s. each.—A THIRD SERIES is in preparation.

Dobson (W. T.).—Poetical Ingenuities and Eccentricities. Post 8vo, cloth limp, 2s. 6d.

Donovan (Dick), Detective Stories by.
Post 8vo, illustrated boards, 2s. each; cloth limp, 2s. 6d. each.
The Man-Hunter. | Wanted.
Caught at Last.
Tracked and Taken.
Who Poisoned Hetty Duncan?
Suspicion Aroused.
A Detective's Triumphs.
In the Grip of the Law.
From Information Received.
Link by Link. | Dark Deeds.
Riddles Read.

Crown 8vo, cloth extra, 3s. 6d. each; post 8vo, illustrated boards, 2s. each; cloth, 2s. 6d. each.
The Man from Manchester. With 23 Illustrations.
Tracked to Doom. With Six full-page Illustrations by GORDON BROWNE.

The Mystery of Jamaica Terrace. Crown 8vo, cloth, 3s. 6d.

Doyle (A. Conan).—The Firm of Girdlestone. Cr. 8vo, cl., 3s. 6d.

Dramatists, The Old. Crown 8vo, cl. ex., with Portraits, 6s. per Vol.
Ben Jonson's Works. With Notes, Critical and Explanatory, and a Biographical Memoir by WILLIAM GIFFORD. Edited by Colonel CUNNINGHAM. Three Vols.
Chapman's Works. Three Vols. Vol. I. contains the Plays complete; Vol. II., Poems and Minor Translations, with an Essay by A. C. SWINBURNE; Vol. III., Translations of the Iliad and Odyssey.
Marlowe's Works. Edited, with Notes, by Colonel CUNNINGHAM. One Vol.
Massinger's Plays. From GIFFORD'S Text. Edited by Colonel CUNNINGHAM. One Vol.

Duncan (Sara Jeannette: Mrs. EVERARD COTES), **Works by.**
Crown 8vo, cloth extra, 7s. 6d. each.
A Social Departure. With 111 Illustrations by F. H. TOWNSEND.
An American Girl in London. With 80 Illustrations by F. H. TOWNSEND.
The Simple Adventures of a Memsahib. With 37 Illustrations by F. H. TOWNSEND.

Crown 8vo, cloth extra, 3s. 6d. each.
A Daughter of To-Day. | Vernon's Aunt. With 47 Illustrations by HAL HURST.

Dyer (T. F. Thiselton).—The Folk-Lore of Plants. Cr. 8vo, cl., 6s.

Early English Poets. Edited, with Introductions and Annotations, by Rev. A. B. GROSART, D.D. Crown 8vo, cloth boards, 6s. per Volume.
Fletcher's (Giles) Complete Poems. One Vol.
Davies' (Sir John) Complete Poetical Works. Two Vols.
Herrick's (Robert) Complete Collected Poems. Three Vols.
Sidney's (Sir Philip) Complete Poetical Works. Three Vols.

Edgcumbe (Sir E. R. Pearce).—Zephyrus: A Holiday in Brazil and on the River Plate. With 41 Illustrations. Crown 8vo, cloth extra, 5s.

Edison, The Life and Inventions of Thomas A. By W. K. L. and ANTONIA DICKSON. With 200 Illustrations by R. F. OUTCALT, &c. Demy 4to, cloth gilt,

Edwardes (Mrs. Annie), Novels by. Post 8vo, illustrated boards, 2s. each.
Archie Lovell. | A Point of Honour.

Edwards (Eliezer).—Words, Facts, and Phrases: A Dictionary of Curious, Quaint, and Out-of-the-Way Matters. Crown 8vo, cloth, 7s. 6d.

Edwards (M. Betham-), Novels by.
Kitty. Post 8vo, boards, 2s.; cloth, 2s. 6d. | Felicia. Post 8vo, illustrated boards, 2s.

Egerton (Rev. J. C., M.A.).— Sussex Folk and Sussex Ways. With Introduction by Rev. Dr. H. WACE, and Four Illustrations. Crown 8vo, cloth extra, 5s.

Eggleston (Edward).—Roxy: A Novel. Post 8vo, illust. boards, 2s.

Englishman's House, The: A Practical Guide for Selecting or Building a House. By C. J. RICHARDSON. Coloured Frontispiece and 534 Illusts. Cr. 8vo, cloth, 7s. 6d.

Ewald (Alex. Charles, F.S.A.), Works by.
The Life and Times of Prince Charles Stuart, Count of Albany (THE YOUNG PRETENDER). With a Portrait. Crown 8vo, cloth extra, 7s. 6d.
Stories from the State Papers. With Autotype Frontispiece. Crown 8vo, cloth, 6s.

Eyes, Our: How to Preserve Them. By JOHN BROWNING. Cr. 8vo, 1s.

Familiar Short Sayings of Great Men. By SAMUEL ARTHUR BENT, A.M. Fifth Edition, Revised and Enlarged. Crown 8vo, cloth extra, 7s. 6d.

Faraday (Michael), Works by. Post 8vo, cloth extra, 4s. 6d. each.
The Chemical History of a Candle: Lectures delivered before a Juvenile Audience. Edited by WILLIAM CROOKES, F.C.S. With numerous Illustrations.
On the Various Forces of Nature, and their Relations to each other. Edited by WILLIAM CROOKES, F.C.S. With Illustrations.

Farrer (J. Anson), Works by.
Military Manners and Customs. Crown 8vo, cloth extra, 6s.
War: Three Essays, reprinted from 'Military Manners and Customs.' Crown 8vo, 1s.; cloth, 1s. 6d.

Fenn (G. Manville), Novels by.
Crown 8vo, cloth extra, 3s. 6d. each; post 8vo, illustrated boards, 2s. each.
The New Mistress. | Witness to the Deed.
The Tiger Lily: A Tale of Two Passions.

The White Virgin. Crown 8vo, cloth extra, 3s. 6d.

Fin-Bec.—The Cupboard Papers: Observations on the Art of Living and Dining. Post 8vo, cloth limp, 2s. 6d.

Fireworks, The Complete Art of Making; or, The Pyrotechnist's Treasury. By THOMAS KENTISH. With 267 Illustrations. Crown 8vo, cloth, 5s.

First Book, My. By WALTER BESANT, JAMES PAYN, W. CLARK RUSSELL, GRANT ALLEN, HALL CAINE, GEORGE R. SIMS, RUDYARD KIPLING, A. CONAN DOYLE, M. E. BRADDON, F. W. ROBINSON, H. RIDER HAGGARD, R. M. BALLANTYNE, I. ZANGWILL, MORLEY ROBERTS, D. CHRISTIE MURRAY, MARY CORELLI, J. K. JEROME, JOHN STRANGE WINTER, BRET HARTE, 'Q.,' ROBERT BUCHANAN, and R. L. STEVENSON. With a Prefatory Story by JEROME K. JEROME, and 185 Illustrations. Small demy 8vo, cloth extra, 7s. 6d.

Fitzgerald (Percy), Works by.
The World Behind the Scenes. Crown 8vo, cloth extra, 3s. 6d.
Little Essays: Passages from the Letters of CHARLES LAMB. Post 8vo, cloth, 2s. 6d.
A Day's Tour: A Journey through France and Belgium. With Sketches. Crown 4to, 1s.
Fatal Zero. Crown 8vo, cloth extra, 3s. 6d.; post 8vo, illustrated boards, 2s.

Post 8vo, illustrated boards, 2s. each.
Bella Donna. | The Lady of Brantome. | The Second Mrs. Tillotson.
Polly. | Never Forgotten. | Seventy-five Brooke Street.

The Life of James Boswell (of Auchinleck). With Illusts. Two Vols., demy 8vo, cloth, 24s.
The Savoy Opera. With 60 Illustrations and Portraits. Crown 8vo, cloth, 3s. 6d.
Sir Henry Irving: Twenty Years at the Lyceum. With Portrait. Crown 8vo, 1s.; cloth, 1s. 6d.

Flammarion (Camille), Works by.
Popular Astronomy: A General Description of the Heavens. Translated by J. ELLARD GORE, F.R.A.S. With Three Plates and 288 Illustrations. Medium 8vo, cloth, 16s.
Urania: A Romance. With 87 Illustrations. Crown 8vo, cloth extra, 5s.

Fletcher's (Giles, B.D.) Complete Poems: Christ's Victorie in Heaven, Christ's Victorie on Earth, Christ's Triumph over Death, and Minor Poems. With Notes by Rev. A. B. GROSART, D.D. Crown 8vo, cloth boards, 6s.

Fonblanque (Albany).—Filthy Lucre. Post 8vo, illust. boards, 2s.

Francillon (R. E.), Novels by. Crown 8vo, cloth extra, 3s. 6d. each; post 8vo, illustrated boards, 2s. each.
One by One. | A Real Queen. | A Dog and his Shadow.
Ropes of Sand. Illustrated.
Post 8vo, illustrated boards, 2s. each.
Queen Cophetua. | Olympia. | Romances of the Law. | King or Knave?
Jack Doyle's Daughter. Crown 8vo, cloth, 3s. 6d.
Esther's Glove. Fcap. 8vo, picture cover, 1s.

Frederic (Harold), Novels by. Post 8vo, illust. boards, 2s. each.
Seth's Brother's Wife. | The Lawton Girl.

French Literature, A History of. By HENRY VAN LAUN. Three Vols., demy 8vo, cloth boards, 7s. 6d. each.

Friswell (Hain).—One of Two: A Novel. Post 8vo, illust. bds., 2s.

Frost (Thomas), Works by. Crown 8vo, cloth extra, 3s. 6d. each.
Circus Life and Circus Celebrities. | Lives of the Conjurers.
The Old Showmen and the Old London Fairs.

Fry's (Herbert) Royal Guide to the London Charities. Edited by JOHN LANE. Published Annually. Crown 8vo, cloth, 1s. 6d.

Gardening Books. Post 8vo, 1s. each; cloth limp. 1s. 6d. each.
A Year's Work in Garden and Greenhouse. By GEORGE GLENNY.
Household Horticulture. By TOM and JANE JERROLD. Illustrated.
The Garden that Paid the Rent. By TOM JERROLD.
My Garden Wild. By FRANCIS G. HEATH. Crown 8vo, cloth extra, 6s.

Gardner (Mrs. Alan).—Rifle and Spear with the Rajpoots: Being the Narrative of a Winter's Travel and Sport in Northern India. With numerous Illustrations by the Author and F. H. TOWNSEND. Demy 4to, half-bound, 21s.

Garrett (Edward).—The Capel Girls: A Novel. Crown 8vo, cloth extra, with two Illustrations, 3s. 6d.; post 8vo, illustrated boards, 2s.

Gaulot (Paul).—The Red Shirts: A Story of the Revolution. Translated by JOHN DE VILLIERS. With a Frontispiece by STANLEY WOOD. Crown 8vo, cloth, 3s. 6d.

Gentleman's Magazine, The. 1s. Monthly. Contains Stories, Articles upon Literature, Science, Biography, and Art, and 'Table Talk' by SYLVANUS URBAN.
⁎ Bound Volumes for recent years kept in stock, 8s. 6d. each. Cases for binding, 2s.

Gentleman's Annual, The. Published Annually in November. 1s.

German Popular Stories. Collected by the Brothers GRIMM and Translated by EDGAR TAYLOR. With Introduction by JOHN RUSKIN, and 22 Steel Plates after GEORGE CRUIKSHANK. Square 8vo, cloth, 6s. 6d.; gilt edges, 7s. 6d.

Gibbon (Charles), Novels by.
Crown 8vo, cloth extra, 3s. 6d. each; post 8vo, illustrated boards, 2s. each.
Robin Gray. Frontispiece. | The Golden Shaft. Frontispiece. | Loving a Dream.
Post 8vo, illustrated boards, 2s. each.
The Flower of the Forest. | In Love and War.
The Dead Heart. | A Heart's Problem.
For Lack of Gold. | By Mead and Stream.
What Will the World Say? | The Braes of Yarrow.
For the King. | A Hard Knot. | Fancy Free. | Of High Degree.
Queen of the Meadow. | In Honour Bound.
In Pastures Green. | Heart's Delight. | Blood-Money.

Gibney (Somerville).—Sentenced! Crown 8vo, 1s.; cloth, 1s. 6d.

Gilbert (W. S.), Original Plays by. In Three Series, 2s. 6d. each.
The FIRST SERIES contains: The Wicked World—Pygmalion and Galatea—Charity—The Princess—The Palace of Truth—Trial by Jury.
The SECOND SERIES: Broken Hearts—Engaged—Sweethearts—Gretchen—Dan'l Druce—Tom Cobb—H.M.S. 'Pinafore'—The Sorcerer—The Pirates of Penzance.
The THIRD SERIES: Comedy and Tragedy—Foggerty's Fairy—Rosencrantz and Guildenstern—Patience—Princess Ida—The Mikado—Ruddigore—The Yeomen of the Guard—The Gondoliers—The Mountebanks—Utopia.

Eight Original Comic Operas written by W. S. GILBERT. Containing: The Sorcerer—H.M.S. 'Pinafore'—The Pirates of Penzance—Iolanthe—Patience—Princess Ida—The Mikado—Trial by Jury. Demy 8vo, cloth limp, 2s. 6d.

The Gilbert and Sullivan Birthday Book: Quotations for Every Day in the Year, selected from Plays by W. S. GILBERT set to Music by Sir A. SULLIVAN. Compiled by ALEX. WATSON. Royal 16mo, Japanese leather, 2s. 6d.

Gilbert (William), Novels by. Post 8vo, illustrated bds., 2s. each.
Dr. Austin's Guests. | James Duke, Costermonger.
The Wizard of the Mountain.

Glanville (Ernest), Novels by.
Crown 8vo, cloth extra, 3s. 6d. each; post 8vo, illustrated boards, 2s. each.
The Lost Heiress: A Tale of Love, Battle, and Adventure. With Two Illustrations by H. NISBET.
The Fossicker: A Romance of Mashonaland. With Two Illustrations by HUME NISBET.
A Fair Colonist. With a Frontispiece by STANLEY WOOD.

The Golden Rock. With a Frontispiece by STANLEY WOOD. Crown 8vo, cloth extra, 3s. 6d.
Kloof Yarns. Crown 8vo, picture cover, 1s.; cloth, 1s. 6d. [Shortly.

Glenny (George).—A Year's Work in Garden and Greenhouse:
Practical Advice as to the Management of the Flower, Fruit, and Frame Garden. Post 8vo, 1s.; cloth, 1s. 6d.

Godwin (William).—Lives of the Necromancers. Post 8vo, cl., 2s.

Golden Treasury of Thought, The: An Encyclopædia of QUOTATIONS. Edited by THEODORE TAYLOR. Crown 8vo, cloth gilt, 7s. 6d.

Gontaut, Memoirs of the Duchesse de (Gouvernante to the Children of France), 1773-1836. With Two Photogravures. Two Vols., demy 8vo, cloth extra, 21s.

Goodman (E. J.).—The Fate of Herbert Wayne. Cr. 8vo, 3s. 6d.

Graham (Leonard).—The Professor's Wife: A Story. Fcp. 8vo, 1s.

Greeks and Romans, The Life of the, described from Antique Monuments. By ERNST GUHL and W. KONER. Edited by Dr. F. HUEFFER. With 545 Illustrations. Large crown 8vo, cloth extra, 7s. 6d.

Greenwood (James), Works by. Crown 8vo, cloth extra, 3s. 6d. each.
The Wilds of London. | Low-Life Deeps.

Greville (Henry), Novels by.
Nikanor. Translated by ELIZA E. CHASE. Post 8vo, illustrated boards, 2s.
A Noble Woman. Crown 8vo, cloth extra, 5s.; post 8vo, illustrated boards, 2s.

Griffith (Cecil).—Corinthia Marazion: A Novel. Crown 8vo, cloth extra, 3s. 6d.; post 8vo, illustrated boards, 2s.

Grundy (Sydney).—The Days of his Vanity: A Passage in the Life of a Young Man. Crown 8vo, cloth extra, 3s. 6d.; post 8vo, illustrated boards, 2s.

Habberton (John, Author of 'Helen's Babies'), **Novels by.**
Post 8vo, illustrated boards, 2s. each; cloth limp, 2s. 6d. each.
Brueton's Bayou. | Country Luck.

Hair, The: Its Treatment in Health, Weakness, and Disease. Translated from the German of Dr. J. PINCUS. Crown 8vo, 1s.; cloth, 1s. 6d.

Hake (Dr. Thomas Gordon), Poems by. Cr. 8vo, cl. ex., 6s. each.
New Symbols. | Legends of the Morrow. | The Serpent Play.
Maiden Ecstasy. Small 4to, cloth extra, 8s.

Hall (Owen).—The Track of a Storm. Crown 8vo, cloth, 6s.

Hall (Mrs. S. C.).—Sketches of Irish Character. With numerous Illustrations on Steel and Wood by MACLISE, GILBERT, HARVEY, and GEORGE CRUIKSHANK. Small demy 8vo, cloth extra, 7s. 6d.

Halliday (Andrew).—Every-day Papers. Post 8vo, boards, 2s.

Handwriting, The Philosophy of. With over 100 Facsimiles and Explanatory Text. By DON FELIX DE SALAMANCA. Post 8vo, cloth limp, 2s. 6d.

Hanky-Panky: Easy and Difficult Tricks, White Magic, Sleight of Hand, &c. Edited by W. H. CREMER. With 200 Illustrations. Crown 8vo, cloth extra, 4s. 6d.

Hardy (Lady Duffus).—Paul Wynter's Sacrifice. Post 8vo, bds., 2s.

Hardy (Thomas).—Under the Greenwood Tree. Crown 8vo, cloth extra, with Portrait and 15 Illustrations, 3s. 6d.; post 8vo, illustrated boards, 2s. cloth limp, 2s. 6d.

Harper (Charles G.), Works by. Demy 8vo, cloth extra, 16s. each.
The Brighton Road. With Photogravure Frontispiece and 90 Illustrations.
From Paddington to Penzance: The Record of a Summer Tramp. With 105 Illustrations.

Harwood (J. Berwick).—The Tenth Earl. Post 8vo, boards, 2s.

Harte's (Bret) Collected Works. Revised by the Author. LIBRARY EDITION, in Eight Volumes, crown 8vo, cloth extra, 6s. each.
Vol. I. COMPLETE POETICAL AND DRAMATIC WORKS. With Steel-plate Portrait.
" II. THE LUCK OF ROARING CAMP—BOHEMIAN PAPERS—AMERICAN LEGENDS.
" III. TALES OF THE ARGONAUTS—EASTERN SKETCHES.
" IV. GABRIEL CONROY. | Vol. V. STORIES—CONDENSED NOVELS, &c.
" VI. TALES OF THE PACIFIC SLOPE.
" VII. TALES OF THE PACIFIC SLOPE—II. With Portrait by JOHN PETTIE, R.A.
" VIII. TALES OF THE PINE AND THE CYPRESS.

The Select Works of Bret Harte, in Prose and Poetry. With Introductory Essay by J. M. BELLEW, Portrait of the Author, and 50 Illustrations. Crown 8vo, cloth extra, 7s. 6d.
Bret Harte's Poetical Works. Printed on hand-made paper. Crown 8vo, buckram, 4s. 6d.
The Queen of the Pirate Isle. With 28 Original Drawings by KATE GREENAWAY, reproduced in Colours by EDMUND EVANS. Small 4to, cloth, 5s.

Crown 8vo, cloth extra, 3s. 6d. each; post 8vo, picture boards, 2s. each.
A Waif of the Plains. With 60 Illustrations by STANLEY L. WOOD.
A Ward of the Golden Gate. With 59 Illustrations by STANLEY L. WOOD.

Crown 8vo, cloth extra, 3s. 6d. each.
A Sappho of Green Springs, &c. With Two Illustrations by HUME NISBET.
Colonel Starbottle's Client, and Some Other People. With a Frontispiece.
Susy: A Novel. With Frontispiece and Vignette by J. A. CHRISTIE.
Sally Dows, &c. With 47 Illustrations by W. D. ALMOND and others.
A Protegee of Jack Hamlin's. With 26 Illustrations by W. SMALL and others.
The Bell-Ringer of Angel's, &c. With 39 Illustrations by DUDLEY HARDY and others
Clarence: A Story of the American War. With Eight Illustrations by A. JULE GOODMAN.

Post 8vo, illustrated boards, 2s. each.
Gabriel Conroy. | **The Luck of Roaring Camp,** &c.
An Heiress of Red Dog, &c. | **Californian Stories.**

Post 8vo, illustrated boards, 2s. each; cloth, 2s. 6d. each.
Flip. | **Maruja.** | **A Phyllis of the Sierras.**

Fcap. 8vo, picture cover, 1s. each.
Snow-Bound at Eagle's. | **Jeff Briggs's Love Story.**

Haweis (Mrs. H. R.), Books by.
The Art of Beauty. With Coloured Frontispiece and 91 Illustrations. Square 8vo, cloth bds., 6s.
The Art of Decoration. With Coloured Frontispiece and 74 Illustrations. Sq. 8vo, cloth bds., 6s.
The Art of Dress. With 32 Illustrations. Post 8vo, 1s.; cloth, 1s. 6d.
Chaucer for Schools. Demy 8vo, cloth limp, 2s. 6d.
Chaucer for Children. With 38 Illustrations (8 Coloured). Crown 4to, cloth extra, 3s. 6d.

Haweis (Rev. H. R., M.A.), Books by.
American Humorists: WASHINGTON IRVING, OLIVER WENDELL HOLMES, JAMES RUSSELL LOWELL, ARTEMUS WARD, MARK TWAIN, and BRET HARTE. Third Edition. Crown 8vo, cloth extra, 6s.
Travel and Talk, 1883, 1893, 1895: America—New Zealand—Tasmania—Ceylon. With Photogravure Frontispieces. Two Vols., crown 8vo, cloth, 21s. [*Shortly.*

Hawthorne (Julian), Novels by.
Crown 8vo, cloth extra, 3s. 6d. each; post 8vo, illustrated boards, 2s. each.
Garth. | **Ellice Quentin.** | **Beatrix Randolph.** With Four Illusts.
Sebastian Strome. | | **David Poindexter's Disappearance.**
Fortune's Fool. | **Dust.** Four Illusts. | **The Spectre of the Camera.**

Post 8vo, illustrated boards, 2s. each.
Miss Cadogna. | **Love—or a Name.**

Mrs. Gainsborough's Diamonds. Fcap. 8vo, illustrated cover, 1s.

Hawthorne (Nathaniel).—Our Old Home. Annotated with Passages from the Author's Note-books, and Illustrated with 31 Photogravures. Two Vols., cr. 8vo, 15s.

Heath (Francis George).—My Garden Wild, and What I Grew There. Crown 8vo, cloth extra, gilt edges, 6s.

Helps (Sir Arthur), Works by. Post 8vo, cloth limp, 2s. 6d. each.
Animals and their Masters. | **Social Pressure.**

Ivan de Biron: A Novel. Crown 8vo, cloth extra, 3s. 6d.; post 8vo, illustrated boards, 2s.

Henderson (Isaac).—Agatha Page: A Novel. Cr. 8vo, cl., 3s. 6d.

Henty (G. A.), Novels by.
Rujub the Juggler. With Eight Illustrations by STANLEY L. WOOD. Crown 8vo, cloth, 3s. 6d.; post 8vo, illustrated boards, 2s.
Dorothy's Double. Crown 8vo, cloth, 3s. 6d.

Herman (Henry).—A Leading Lady. Post 8vo, bds., 2s.; cl., 2s. 6d.

Herrick's (Robert) Hesperides, Noble Numbers, and Complete Collected Poems. With Memorial-Introduction and Notes by the Rev. A. B. GROSART, D.D., Steel Portrait, &c. Three Vols., crown 8vo, cloth boards, 18s.

Hertzka (Dr. Theodor).—Freeland: A Social Anticipation. Translated by ARTHUR RANSOM. Crown 8vo, cloth extra, 6s.

Hesse-Wartegg (Chevalier Ernst von).— Tunis: The Land and the People. With 22 Illustrations. Crown 8vo, cloth extra, 3s. 6d.

Hill (Headon).—Zambra the Detective. Post 8vo, bds., 2s.; cl., 2s. 6d.

Hill (John), Works by.
Treason-Felony. Post 8vo, boards, 2s. | The Common Ancestor. Cr. 8vo, cloth, 3s. 6d.

Hindley (Charles), Works by.
Tavern Anecdotes and Sayings: Including Reminiscences connected with Coffee Houses, Clubs, &c. With Illustrations. Crown 8vo, cloth extra, 3s. 6d.
The Life and Adventures of a Cheap Jack. Crown 8vo, cloth extra, 3s. 6d.

Hodges (Sydney).—When Leaves were Green. 3 vols., 15s. net.

Hoey (Mrs. Cashel).—The Lover's Creed. Post 8vo, boards, 2s.

Hollingshead (John).—Niagara Spray. Crown 8vo, 1s.

Holmes (Gordon, M.D.)—The Science of Voice Production and Voice Preservation. Crown 8vo, 1s.; cloth, 1s. 6d.

Holmes (Oliver Wendell), Works by.
The Autocrat of the Breakfast-Table. Illustrated by J. GORDON THOMSON. Post 8vo, cloth limp, 2s. 6d.— Another Edition, post 8vo, cloth, 2s.
The Autocrat of the Breakfast-Table and The Professor at the Breakfast-Table. In One Vol. Post 8vo, half-bound, 2s.

Hood's (Thomas) Choice Works in Prose and Verse. With Life of the Author, Portrait, and 200 Illustrations. Crown 8vo, cloth extra, 7s. 6d.
Hood's Whims and Oddities. With 85 Illustrations. Post 8vo, half-bound, 2s.

Hood (Tom).—From Nowhere to the North Pole: A Noah's Arkæological Narrative. With 25 Illustrations by W. BRUNTON and E. C. BARNES. Cr. 8vo, cloth, 6s.

Hook's (Theodore) Choice Humorous Works; including his Ludicrous Adventures, Bons Mots, Puns, and Hoaxes. With Life of the Author, Portraits, Facsimiles, and Illustrations. Crown 8vo, cloth extra, 7s. 6d.

Hooper (Mrs. Geo.).—The House of Raby. Post 8vo, boards, 2s.

Hopkins (Tighe).—"'Twixt Love and Duty.' Post 8vo, boards, 2s.

Horne (R. Hengist).— Orion: An Epic Poem. With Photograph Portrait by SUMMERS. Tenth Edition. Crown 8vo, cloth extra, 7s.

Hungerford (Mrs., Author of 'Molly Bawn'), **Novels by.**
Post 8vo, illustrated boards, 2s. each; cloth limp, 2s. 6d. each.
A Maiden All Forlorn. | In Durance Vile. | A Mental Struggle.
Marvel. | A Modern Circe. |

Crown 8vo, cloth extra, 3s. 6d. each; post 8vo, illustrated boards, 2s. each; cloth limp, 2s. 6d. each.
Lady Verner's Flight. | The Red-House Mystery.

The Three Graces. With 6 Illustrations. Crown 8vo, cloth extra, 3s. 6d. [Shortly.
The Professor's Experiment. Three Vols., crown 8vo, 15s. net.
A Point of Conscience. Three Vols., crown 8vo, 15s. net.

Hunt's (Leigh) Essays: A Tale for a Chimney Corner, &c. Edited by EDMUND OLLIER. Post 8vo, half-bound, 2s.

Hunt (Mrs. Alfred), Novels by.
Crown 8vo, cloth extra, 3s. 6d. each; post 8vo, illustrated boards, 2s. each.
The Leaden Casket. | Self-Condemned. | That Other Person.
Thornicroft's Model. Post 8vo, boards, 2s. | Mrs. Juliet. Crown 8vo, cloth extra, 3s. 6d.

Hutchison (W. M.).—Hints on Colt-breaking. With 25 Illustrations. Crown 8vo, cloth extra, 3s. 6d.

Hydrophobia: An Account of M. PASTEUR's System; The Technique of his Method, and Statistics. By RENAUD SUZOR, M.B. Crown 8vo, cloth extra, 6s.

Hyne (C. J. Cutcliffe).— Honour of Thieves. Cr. 8vo, cloth, 3s. 6d.

Idler (The): An Illustrated Magazine. Edited by J. K. JEROME. 1s. Monthly. The First EIGHT VOLS. are now ready, cloth extra, 5s. each; Cases for Binding, 1s. 6d. each.

CHATTO & WINDUS, PUBLISHERS, PICCADILLY. 13

Impressions (The) of Aureole. Crown 8vo, printed on blush-rose paper and handsomely bound, 6s.

Indoor Paupers. By ONE OF THEM. Crown 8vo, 1s.; cloth, 1s. 6d.

Ingelow (Jean).—Fated to be Free. Post 8vo, illustrated bds., 2s.

Innkeeper's Handbook (The) and Licensed Victualler's Manual. By J. TREVOR-DAVIES. Crown 8vo, 1s.; cloth, 1s. 6d.

Irish Wit and Humour, Songs of. Collected and Edited by A. PERCEVAL GRAVES. Post 8vo, cloth limp, 2s. 6d.

Irving (Sir Henry): A Record of over Twenty Years at the Lyceum. By PERCY FITZGERALD. With Portrait. Crown 8vo, 1s.; cloth, 1s. 6d.

James (C. T. C.).— A Romance of the Queen's Hounds. Post 8vo, picture cover, 1s.; cloth limp, 1s. 6d.

Jameson (William).—My Dead Self. Post 8vo, bds., 2s.; cl., 2s. 6d.

Japp (Alex. H., LL.D.).—Dramatic Pictures, &c. Cr. 8vo, cloth, 5s.

Jay (Harriett), Novels by. Post 8vo, illustrated boards, 2s. each.
The Dark Colleen. | The Queen of Connaught.

Jefferies (Richard), Works by. Post 8vo, cloth limp, 2s. 6d. each.
Nature near London. | The Life of the Fields. | The Open Air.
*** Also the HAND-MADE PAPER EDITION, crown 8vo, buckram, gilt top, 6s. each.

The Eulogy of Richard Jefferies. By Sir WALTER BESANT. With a Photograph Portrait. Crown 8vo, cloth extra, 6s.

Jennings (Henry J.), Works by.
Curiosities of Criticism. Post 8vo, cloth limp, 2s. 6d.
Lord Tennyson: A Biographical Sketch. With Portrait. Post 8vo, 1s.; cloth, 1s. 6d.

Jerome (Jerome K.), Books by.
Stageland. With 64 Illustrations by J. BERNARD PARTRIDGE. Fcap. 4to, picture cover, 1s.
John Ingerfield, &c. With 9 Illusts. by A. S. BOYD and JOHN GULICH. Fcap. 8vo, pic. cov. 1s. 6d.
The Prude's Progress: A Comedy by J. K. JEROME and EDEN PHILLPOTTS. Cr. 8vo, 1s. 6d.

Jerrold (Douglas).—The Barber's Chair; and The Hedgehog Letters. Post 8vo, printed on laid paper and half-bound, 2s.

Jerrold (Tom), Works by. Post 8vo, 1s. ea.; cloth limp, 1s. 6d. each.
The Garden that Paid the Rent.
Household Horticulture: A Gossip about Flowers. Illustrated.

Jesse (Edward).—Scenes and Occupations of a Country Life. Post 8vo, cloth limp, 2s.

Jones (William, F.S.A.), Works by. Cr. 8vo, cl. extra, 7s. 6d. each.
Finger-Ring Lore: Historical, Legendary, and Anecdotal. With nearly 300 Illustrations. Second Edition, Revised and Enlarged.
Credulities, Past and Present. Including the Sea and Seamen, Miners, Talismans, Word and Letter Divination, Exorcising and Blessing of Animals, Birds, Eggs, Luck, &c. With Frontispiece.
Crowns and Coronations: A History of Regalia. With 100 Illustrations.

Jonson's (Ben) Works. With Notes Critical and Explanatory, and a Biographical Memoir by WILLIAM GIFFORD. Edited by Colonel CUNNINGHAM. Three Vols. crown 8vo, cloth extra, 6s. each.

Josephus, The Complete Works of. Translated by WHISTON. Containing 'The Antiquities of the Jews' and 'The Wars of the Jews.' With 52 Illustrations and Maps. Two Vols., demy 8vo, half-bound, 12s. 6d.

Kempt (Robert).—Pencil and Palette: Chapters on Art and Artists. Post 8vo, cloth limp, 2s. 6d.

Kershaw (Mark). — Colonial Facts and Fictions: Humorous Sketches. Post 8vo, illustrated boards, 2s.; cloth, 2s. 6d.

Keyser (Arthur).—Cut by the Mess. Crown 8vo, 1s.; cloth, 1s. 6d.

King (R. Ashe), Novels by. Cr. 8vo, cl., 3s. 6d. ea.; post 8vo, bds., 2s. ea.
A Drawn Game. | 'The Wearing of the Green.'

Post 8vo, illustrated boards, 2s. each.
Passion's Slave. | Bell Barry.

**Knight (William, M.R.C.S., and Edward, L.R.C.P.). — The
Patient's Vade Mecum: How to Get Most Benefit from Medical Advice.** Cr. 8vo, 1s.; cl., 1s. 6d.

Knights (The) of the Lion: A Romance of the Thirteenth Century.
Edited, with an Introduction, by the MARQUESS OF LORNE, K.T. Crown 8vo, cloth extra, 6s.

Lamb's (Charles) Complete Works in Prose and Verse, including
'Poetry for Children' and 'Prince Dorus.' Edited, with Notes and Introduction, by R. H. SHEP-
HERD. With Two Portraits and Facsimile of the 'Essay on RoastPig.' Crown 8vo, half-bd., 7s. 6d.
The Essays of Elia. Post 8vo, printed on laid paper and half-bound, 2s.
Little Essays: Sketches and Characters by CHARLES LAMB, selected from his Letters by PERCY
FITZGERALD. Post 8vo, cloth limp, 2s. 6d.
The Dramatic Essays of Charles Lamb. With Introduction and Notes by BRANDER MAT-
THEWS, and Steel-plate Portrait. Fcap. 8vo, half-bound, 2s. 6d.

Landor (Walter Savage).—Citation and Examination of William
Shakspeare, &c., before Sir Thomas Lucy, touching Deer-stealing, 19th September, 1582. To which
is added, **A Conference of Master Edmund Spenser** with the Earl of Essex, touching the
State of Ireland, 1595. Fcap. 8vo, half-Roxburghe, 2s. 6d.

Lane (Edward William).—The Thousand and One Nights, com-
monly called in England **The Arabian Nights' Entertainments.** Translated from the Arabic,
with Notes. Illustrated with many hundred Engravings from Designs by HARVEY. Edited by EDWARD
STANLEY POOLE. With Preface by STANLEY LANE-POOLE. Three Vols., demy 8vo, cloth, 7s. 6d. ea.

Larwood (Jacob), Works by.
The Story of the London Parks. With Illustrations. Crown 8vo, cloth extra, 3s. 6d.
Anecdotes of the Clergy. Post 8vo, laid paper, half-bound, 2s.

Post 8vo, cloth limp, 2s. 6d. each.
Forensic Anecdotes. | **Theatrical Anecdotes.**

Lehmann (R. C.), Works by. Post 8vo, 1s. each; cloth, 1s. 6d. each.
Harry Fludyer at Cambridge.
Conversational Hints for Young Shooters: A Guide to Polite Talk.

Leigh (Henry S.), Works by.
Carols of Cockayne. Printed on hand-made paper, bound in buckram, 5s.
Jeux d'Esprit. Edited by HENRY S. LEIGH. Post 8vo, cloth limp, 2s. 6d.

Leland (C. Godfrey). — A Manual of Mending and Repairing.
With Diagrams. Crown 8vo, cloth, 5s. [Shortly.

Lepelletier (Edmond). — Madame Sans-Gène. Translated from
the French by JOHN DE VILLIERS. Crown 8vo, cloth extra, 3s. 6d.

Leys (John).—The Lindsays: A Romance. Post 8vo, illust. bds., 2s.

Lindsay (Harry).—Rhoda Roberts: A Welsh Mining Story. Crown
8vo, cloth, 3s. 6d.

Linton (E. Lynn), Works by.
Crown 8vo, cloth extra, 3s. 6d. each; post 8vo, illustrated boards, 2s. each.
Patricia Kemball. | **Ione.** | **Under which Lord?** With 12 Illustrations.
The Atonement of Leam Dundas. | **'My Love!'** | **Sowing the Wind.**
The World Well Lost. With 12 Illusts. | **Paston Carew,** Millionaire and Miser.
The One Too Many.

Post 8vo, illustrated boards, 2s. each.
The Rebel of the Family. | **With a Silken Thread.**

Post 8vo, cloth limp, 2s. 6d. each.
Witch Stories. | **Ourselves:** Essays on Women.
Freeshooting: Extracts from the Works of Mrs. LYNN LINTON.

Lucy (Henry W.).—Gideon Fleyce: A Novel. Crown 8vo, cloth
extra, 3s. 6d.; post 8vo, illustrated boards, 2s.

Macalpine (Avery), Novels by.
Teresa Itasca. Crown 8vo, cloth extra, 1s.
Broken Wings. With Six Illustrations by W. J. HENNESSY. Crown 8vo, cloth extra, 6s.

MacColl (Hugh), Novels by.
Mr. Stranger's Sealed Packet. Post 8vo, illustrated boards, 2s.
Ednor Whitlock. Crown 8vo, cloth extra, 6s.

Macdonell (Agnes).—Quaker Cousins. Post 8vo, boards, 2s.

MacGregor (Robert).—Pastimes and Players: Notes on Popular
Games. Post 8vo, cloth limp, 2s. 6d.

Mackay (Charles, LL.D.). — Interludes and Undertones; or,
Music at Twilight. Crown 8vo, cloth extra, 6s.

CHATTO &. WINDUS, PUBLISHERS, PICCADILLY. 15

McCarthy (Justin, M.P.), Works by.
A History of Our Own Times, from the Accession of Queen Victoria to the General Election of 1880. Four Vols., demy 8vo, cloth extra, 12s. each.—Also a POPULAR EDITION, in Four Vols., crown 8vo, cloth extra, 6s. each.—And the JUBILEE EDITION, with an Appendix of Events to the end of 1886, in Two Vols., large crown 8vo, cloth extra, 7s. 6d. each.
A Short History of Our Own Times. One Vol., crown 8vo, cloth extra, 6s.—Also a CHEAP POPULAR EDITION, post 8vo, cloth limp, 2s. 6d.
A History of the Four Georges. Four Vols., demy 8vo, cl. ex., 12s. each. [Vols. I. & II. ready.

Crown 8vo, cloth extra, 3s. 6d. each; post 8vo, illustrated boards, 2s. each; cloth limp, 2s. 6d. each.

The Waterdale Neighbours.
My Enemy's Daughter.
A Fair Saxon.
Linley Rochford.
Dear Lady Disdain.
Miss Misanthrope. With 12 Illustrations.
Donna Quixote. With 12 Illustrations.
The Comet of a Season.
Maid of Athens. With 12 Illustrations.
Camiola: A Girl with a Fortune.
The Dictator.
Red Diamonds.

'The Right Honourable.' By JUSTIN MCCARTHY, M.P., and Mrs. CAMPBELL PRAED. Crown 8vo, cloth extra, 6s.

McCarthy (Justin Huntly), Works by.
The French Revolution. (Constituent Assembly, 1789-91). Four Vols., demy 8vo, cloth extra, 12s. each. Vols. I. & II. ready; Vols. III. & IV. in the press.
An Outline of the History of Ireland. Crown 8vo, 1s.; cloth, 1s. 6d.
Ireland Since the Union: Sketches of Irish History, 1798-1886. Crown 8vo, cloth, 6s.

Hafiz in London: Poems. Small 8vo, gold cloth, 3s. 6d.

Our Sensation Novel. Crown 8vo, picture cover, 1s.; cloth limp, 1s. 6d.
Doom: An Atlantic Episode. Crown 8vo, picture cover, 1s.
Dolly: A Sketch. Crown 8vo, picture cover, 1s.; cloth limp, 1s. 6d.
Lily Lass: A Romance. Crown 8vo, picture cover, 1s.; cloth limp, 1s. 6d.
The Thousand and One Days. With Two Photogravures. Two Vols., crown 8vo, half-bd., 12s.
A London Legend. Crown 8vo, cloth, 3s. 6d.

MacDonald (George, LL.D.), Books by.
Works of Fancy and Imagination. Ten Vols., 16mo, cloth, gilt edges, in cloth case, 21s.; or the Volumes may be had separately, in Grolier cloth, at 2s. 6d. each.
Vol. I. WITHIN AND WITHOUT.—THE HIDDEN LIFE.
" II. THE DISCIPLE.—THE GOSPEL WOMEN.—BOOK OF SONNETS.—ORGAN SONGS.
" III. VIOLIN SONGS.—SONGS OF THE DAYS AND NIGHTS.—A BOOK OF DREAMS.—ROADSIDE POEMS.—POEMS FOR CHILDREN.
" IV. PARABLES.—BALLADS.—SCOTCH SONGS.
" V. & VI. PHANTASTES: A Faerie Romance. | Vol. VII. THE PORTENT.
" VIII. THE LIGHT PRINCESS.—THE GIANT'S HEART.—SHADOWS.
" IX. CROSS PURPOSES.—THE GOLDEN KEY.—THE CARASOYN.—LITTLE DAYLIGHT.
" X. THE CRUEL PAINTER.—THE WOW O' RIVVEN.—THE CASTLE.—THE BROKEN SWORDS. —THE GRAY WOLF.—UNCLE CORNELIUS.

Poetical Works of George MacDonald. Collected and Arranged by the Author. Two Vols. crown 8vo, buckram, 12s.
A Threefold Cord. Edited by GEORGE MACDONALD. Post 8vo, cloth, 5s.

Phantastes: A Faerie Romance. With 25 Illustrations by J. BELL. Crown 8vo, cloth extra, 3s. 6d.
Heather and Snow: A Novel. Crown 8vo, cloth extra, 3s. 6d.; post 8vo, illustrated boards, 2s.
Lilith: A Romance. SECOND EDITION. Crown 8vo, cloth extra, 6s.

Maclise Portrait Gallery (The) of Illustrious Literary Characters: 85 Portraits
by DANIEL MACLISE; with Memoirs—Biographical, Critical, Bibliographical, and Anecdotal—illustrative of the Literature of the former half of the Present Century, by WILLIAM BATES, B.A. Crown 8vo, cloth extra, 7s. 6d.

Macquoid (Mrs.), Works by. Square 8vo, cloth extra, 6s. each.
In the Ardennes. With 50 Illustrations by THOMAS R. MACQUOID.
Pictures and Legends from Normandy and Brittany. 34 Illusts. by T. R. MACQUOID.
Through Normandy. With 92 Illustrations by T. R. MACQUOID, and a Map.
Through Brittany. With 35 Illustrations by T. R. MACQUOID, and a Map.
About Yorkshire. With 67 Illustrations by T. R. MACQUOID.

Post 8vo, illustrated boards, 2s. each.
The Evil Eye, and other Stories. | **Lost Rose,** and other Stories.

Magician's Own Book, The: Performances with Eggs, Hats, &c.
Edited by W. H. CREMER. With 200 Illustrations. Crown 8vo, cloth extra, 4s. 6d.

Magic Lantern, The, and its Management : Including full Practical
Directions. By T. C. HEPWORTH. With 10 Illustrations. Crown 8vo, 1s.; cloth, 1s. 6d.

Magna Charta : An Exact Facsimile of the Original in the British
Museum, 3 feet by 2 feet, with Arms and Seals emblazoned in Gold and Colours, 5s.

Mallory (Sir Thomas). — Mort d'Arthur: The Stories of King
Arthur and of the Knights of the Round Table. (A Selection.) Edited by B. MONTGOMERIE RANKING. Post 8vo, cloth limp, 2s.

CHATTO & WINDUS, PUBLISHERS, PICCADILLY.

Mallock (W. H.), Works by.
The New Republic. Post 8vo, picture cover, 2s.; cloth limp, 2s. 6d.
The New Paul & Virginia: Positivism on an Island. Post 8vo, cloth, 2s. 6d.
A Romance of the Nineteenth Century. Crown 8vo, cloth 6s.; pos 8vo, illust. boards, 2s.
Poems. Small 4to, parchment, 8s.
Is Life Worth Living? Crown 8vo, cloth extra, 6s.

Mark Twain, Books by. Crown 8vo, cloth extra, 7s. 6d. each.
The Choice Works of Mark Twain. Revised and Corrected throughout by the Author. With Life, Portrait, and numerous Illustrations.
Roughing It; and The Innocents at Home. With 200 Illustrations by F. A. FRASER.
Mark Twain's Library of Humour. With 197 Illustrations.

Crown 8vo, cloth extra (illustrated), 7s. 6d. each; post 8vo, illustrated boards, 2s. each.
The Innocents Abroad; or, The New Pilgrim's Progress. With 234 Illustrations. (The Two Shilling Edition is entitled Mark Twain's Pleasure Trip.)
The Gilded Age. By MARK TWAIN and C. D. WARNER. With 212 Illustrations.
The Adventures of Tom Sawyer. With 111 Illustrations.
A Tramp Abroad. With 314 Illustrations.
The Prince and the Pauper. With 190 Illustrations.
Life on the Mississippi. With 300 Illustrations.
The Adventures of Huckleberry Finn. With 174 Illustrations by E. W. KEMBLE.
A Yankee at the Court of King Arthur. With 220 Illustrations by DAN BEARD.

Crown 8vo, cloth extra, 3s. 6d. each.
The American Claimant. With 81 Illustrations by HAL HURST and others.
Tom Sawyer Abroad. With 26 Illustrations by DAN. BEARD.
Pudd'nhead Wilson. With Portrait and Six Illlustrations by LOUIS LOEB.
Tom Sawyer, Detective, &c. With numerous Illustrations. [Shortly.

The £1,000,000 Bank-Note. Crown 8vo, cloth, 3s. 6d.; post 8vo, picture boards 2s.

Post 8vo, illustrated boards, 2s. each.
The Stolen White Elephant. | Mark Twain's Sketches.

Marks (H. S., R.A.), Pen and Pencil Sketches by. With Four Photogravures and 126 Illustrations. Two Vols. demy 8vo, cloth, 32s.

Marlowe's Works. Including his Translations. Edited, with Notes and Introductions, by Colonel CUNNINGHAM. Crown 8vo, cloth extra, 6s.

Marryat (Florence), Novels by. Post 8vo, illust. boards, 2s. each.
A Harvest of Wild Oats. | Fighting the Air.
Open ! Sesame ! | Written in Fire.

Massinger's Plays. From the Text of WILLIAM GIFFORD, Edited by Col. CUNNINGHAM. Crown 8vo, cloth extra, 6s.

Masterman (J.).—Half-a-Dozen Daughters. Post 8vo, boards, 2s.

Matthews (Brander).—A Secret of the Sea, &c. Post 8vo, illustrated boards, 2s.; cloth limp, 2s. 6d.

Mayhew (Henry).—London Characters, and the Humorous Side of London Life. With numerous Illustrations. Crown 8vo, cloth, 3s. 6d.

Meade (L. T.), Novels by.
A Soldier of Fortune. Crown 8vo, cloth, 3s. 6d.; post 8vo, illustrated boards, 2s.
In an Iron Grip. Crown 8vo, cloth, 3s. 6d.
The Voice of the Charmer. Three Vols., 15s. net.

Merrick (Leonard).—The Man who was Good. Post 8vo, illustrated boards, 2s.

Mexican Mustang (On a), through Texas to the Rio Grande. By A. E. SWEET and J. ARMOY KNOX With 265 Illustrations. Crown 8vo, cloth extra, 7s. 6d.

Middlemass (Jean), Novels by. Post 8vo, illust. boards, 2s. each.
Touch and Go. | Mr. Dorillion.

Miller (Mrs. F. Fenwick).—Physiology for the Young; or, The House of Life. With numerous Illustrations. Post 8vo, cloth limp, 2s. 6d.

Milton (J. L.), Works by. Post 8vo, 1s. each; cloth, 1s. 6d. each.
The Hygiene of the Skin. With Directions for Diet, Soaps, Baths, Wines, &c.
The Bath in Diseases of the Skin.
The Laws of Life, and their Relation to Diseases of the Skin.

Minto (Wm.).—Was She Good or Bad? Cr. 8vo, 1s.; cloth, 1s. 6d.

CHATTO & WINDUS, PUBLISHERS, PICCADILLY.   17

Mitford (Bertram), Novels by. Crown 8vo, cloth extra, 3s. 6d. each.
The Gun-Runner: A Romance of Zululand. With a Frontispiece by STANLEY L. WOOD.
The Luck of Gerard Ridgeley. With a Frontispiece by STANLEY L. WOOD.
The King's Assegai. With Six full-page Illustrations by STANLEY L. WOOD.
Renshaw Fanning's Quest. With a Frontispiece by STANLEY L. WOOD.

Molesworth (Mrs.), Novels by.
Hathercourt Rectory. Post 8vo, illustrated boards, 2s.
That Girl in Black. Crown 8vo, cloth, 1s. 6d.

Moncrieff (W. D. Scott-).—The Abdication: An Historical Drama.
With Seven Etchings by JOHN PETTIE, W. Q. ORCHARDSON, J. MACWHIRTER, COLIN HUNTER, R. MACBETH and TOM GRAHAM. Imperial 4to, buckram, 21s.

Moore (Thomas), Works by.
The Epicurean; and Alciphron. Post 8vo, half-bound, 2s.
Prose and Verse; including Suppressed Passages from the MEMOIRS OF LORD BYRON. Edited by R. H. SHEPHERD. With Portrait. Crown 8vo, cloth extra, 7s. 6d.

Muddock (J. E.) Stories by.
Stories Weird and Wonderful. Post 8vo, illustrated boards, 2s.; cloth, 2s. 6d.
The Dead Man's Secret. With Frontispiece by F. BARNARD. Post 8vo, picture boards, 2s.
From the Bosom of the Deep. Post 8vo, illustrated boards, 2s.
Maid Marian and Robin Hood. With 12 Illusts. by STANLEY WOOD. Cr. 8vo, cloth extra, 3s. 6d.
Basile the Jester. With Frontispiece by STANLEY WOOD. Crown 8vo, cloth, 3s. 6d.

Murray (D. Christie), Novels by.
Crown 8vo, cloth extra, 3s. 6d. each; post 8vo, illustrated boards, 2s. each.

A Life's Atonement.	A Model Father.	First Person Singular.
Joseph's Coat. 12 Illusts.	Old Blazer's Hero.	Bob Martin's Little Girl.
Coals of Fire. 3 Illusts.	Cynic Fortune. Frontisp.	Time's Revenges.
Val Strange.	By the Gate of the Sea.	A Wasted Crime.
Hearts.	A Bit of Human Nature.	In Direst Peril.
The Way of the World.		

Mount Despair, &c. With Frontispiece by GRENVILLE MANTON. Crown 8vo, cloth, 3s. 6d.
The Making of a Novelist: An Experiment in Autobiography. With a Collotype Portrait and Vignette. Crown 8vo, art linen, 6s.

Murray (D. Christie) and Henry Herman, Novels by.
Crown 8vo, cloth extra, 3s. 6d. each; post 8vo, illustrated boards, 2s. each.
One Traveller Returns. | The Bishops' Bible.
Paul Jones's Alias, &c. With Illustrations by A. FORESTIER and G. NICOLET.

Murray (Henry), Novels by.
Post 8vo, illustrated boards, 2s. each; cloth, 2s. 6d. each.
A Game of Bluff. | A Song of Sixpence.

Newbolt (Henry).—Taken from the Enemy. Fcp. 8vo, cloth, 1s. 6d.

Nisbet (Hume), Books by.
'Bail Up.' Crown 8vo, cloth extra, 3s. 6d.; post 8vo, illustrated boards, 2s.
Dr. Bernard St. Vincent. Post 8vo, illustrated boards, 2s.

Lessons in Art. With 21 Illustrations. Crown 8vo, cloth extra, 2s. 6d.
Where Art Begins. With 27 Illustrations. Square 8vo, cloth extra, 7s. 6d.

Norris (W. E.), Novels by. Crown 8vo, cloth, 3s. 6d. each.
Saint Ann's. | Billy Bellew. With Frontispiece. [Shortly.

O'Hanlon (Alice), Novels by. Post 8vo, illustrated boards, 2s. each.
The Unforeseen. | Chance? or Fate?

Ouida, Novels by. Cr. 8vo, cl., 3s. 6d. ea.; post 8vo, illust. bds., 2s. ea.

Held in Bondage.	Folle-Farine.	Moths.	Pipistrello.
Tricotrin.	A Dog of Flanders.	In Maremma.	Wanda.
Strathmore.	Pascarel.	Signa.	Bimbi.	Syrlin.
Chandos.	Two Wooden Shoes.	Frescoes.	Othmar.
Cecil Castlemaine's Gage	In a Winter City.	Princess Napraxine.
Under Two Flags.	Ariadne.	Friendship.	Guilderoy.	Ruffino.
Puck.	Idalia.	A Village Commune.	Two Offenders.

Square 8vo, cloth extra, 5s. each.
Bimbi. With Nine Illustrations by EDMUND H. GARRETT.
A Dog of Flanders, &c. With Six Illustrations by EDMUND H. GARRETT.

Santa Barbara, &c. Square 8vo, cloth, 6s.; crown 8vo, cloth, 3s. 6d.; post 8vo, illustrated boards, 2s.
Under Two Flags. POPULAR EDITION. Medium 8vo, 6d.; cloth, 1s. [Shortly.

Wisdom, Wit, and Pathos, selected from the Works of OUIDA by F. SYDNEY MORRIS. Post 8vo, cloth extra, 5s.—CHEAP EDITION, illustrated boards, 2s.

Ohnet (Georges), Novels by. Post 8vo, illustrated boards, 2s. each.
Doctor Rameau. | A Last Love.

A Weird Gift. Crown 8vo, cloth, 3s. 6d.; post 8vo, picture boards, 2s.

Oliphant (Mrs.), Novels by. Post 8vo, illustrated boards, 2s. each.
The Primrose Path. | Whiteladies.
The Greatest Heiress in England.

O'Reilly (Mrs.).—Phœbe's Fortunes. Post 8vo, illust. boards, 2s.

Page (H. A.), Works by.
Thoreau: His Life and Aims. With Portrait. Post 8vo, cloth limp, 2s. 6d.
Animal Anecdotes. Arranged on a New Principle. Crown 8vo, cloth extra, 5s.

Pandurang Hari; or, Memoirs of a Hindoo. With Preface by Sir BARTLE FRERE. Crown 8vo, cloth, 3s. 6d.; post 8vo, illustrated boards, 2s.

Pascal's Provincial Letters. A New Translation, with Historical Introduction and Notes by T. M'CRIE, D.D. Post 8vo, cloth limp, 2s.

Paul (Margaret A.).—Gentle and Simple. Crown 8vo, cloth, with Frontispiece by HELEN PATERSON, 3s. 6d.; post 8vo, illustrated boards, 2s.

Payn (James), Novels by.
Crown 8vo, cloth extra, 3s. 6d. each; post 8vo, illustrated boards, 2s. each.

Lost Sir Massingberd. | Holiday Tasks.
Walter's Word. | The Canon's Ward. With Portrait.
Less Black than We're Painted. | The Talk of the Town. With 12 Illusts.
By Proxy. | For Cash Only. | Glow-Worm Tales.
High Spirits. | The Mystery of Mirbridge.
Under One Roof. | The Word and the Will.
A Confidential Agent. With 10 Illusts. | The Burnt Million.
A Grape from a Thorn. With 12 Illusts. | Sunny Stories. | A Trying Patient.

Post 8vo, illustrated boards, 2s. each.

Humorous Stories. | From Exile. | Found Dead.
The Foster Brothers. | Gwendoline's Harvest.
The Family Scapegrace. | A Marine Residence.
Married Beneath Him. | Mirk Abbey.
Bentinck's Tutor. | Some Private Views.
A Perfect Treasure. | Not Wooed, But Won.
A County Family. | Two Hundred Pounds Reward.
Like Father, Like Son. | The Best of Husbands.
A Woman's Vengeance. | Halves.
Carlyon's Year. | Cecil's Tryst. | Fallen Fortunes.
Murphy's Master. | What He Cost Her.
At Her Mercy. | Kit: A Memory.
The Clyffards of Clyffe. | A Prince of the Blood.

In Peril and Privation. With 17 Illustrations. Crown 8vo, cloth, 3s. 6d.
Notes from the 'News.' Crown 8vo, portrait cover, 1s.; cloth, 1s. 6d.

Pennell (H. Cholmondeley), Works by. Post 8vo, cloth, 2s. 6d. ea.
Puck on Pegasus. With Illustrations.
Pegasus Re-Saddled. With Ten full-page Illustrations by G. DU MAURIER.
The Muses of Mayfair: Vers de Société. Selected by H. C. PENNELL.

Phelps (E. Stuart), Works by. Post 8vo, 1s. ea.; cloth, 1s. 6d. ea.
Beyond the Gates. | An Old Maid's Paradise. | Burglars in Paradise.

Jack the Fisherman. Illustrated by C. W. REED. Crown 8vo, 1s.; cloth, 1s. 6d.

Phil May's Sketch-Book. Containing 50 full-page Drawings. Imp. 4to, art canvas, gilt top, 10s. 6d.

Pirkis (C. L.), Novels by.
Trooping with Crows. Fcap. 8vo, picture cover, 1s.
Lady Lovelace. Post 8vo, illustrated boards, 2s.

Planche (J. R.), Works by.
The Pursuivant of Arms. With Six Plates and 209 Illustrations. Crown 8vo, cloth, 7s. 6d.
Songs and Poems, 1819-1879. With Introduction by Mrs. MACKARNESS. Crown 8vo, cloth, 6s.

Plutarch's Lives of Illustrious Men. With Notes and a Life of Plutarch by JOHN and WM. LANGHORNE, and Portraits. Two Vols., demy 8vo, half-bound 10s. 6d.

Poe's (Edgar Allan) Choice Works in Prose and Poetry. With Introduction by CHARLES BAUDELAIRE, Portrait and Facsimiles. Crown 8vo, cloth, 7s. 6d.
The Mystery of Marie Roget, &c. Post 8vo, illustrated boards, 2s.

CHATTO & WINDUS, PUBLISHERS, PICCADILLY.   19

Pope's Poetical Works. Post 8vo, cloth limp, 2s.

Praed (Mrs. Campbell), Novels by. Post 8vo, illust. bds., 2s. each.
The Romance of a Station. | The Soul of Countess Adrian.
Crown 8vo, cloth, 3s. 6d. each; post 8vo, boards, 2s. each.
Outlaw and Lawmaker. | Christina Chard. With Frontispiece by W. PAGET.
Mrs. Tregaskiss. Three Vols., crown 8vo, 15s. net.

Price (E. C.), Novels by.
Crown 8vo, cloth extra, 3s. 6d. each; post 8vo, illustrated boards, 2s. each.
Valentina. | The Foreigners. | Mrs. Lancaster's Rival.
Gerald. Post 8vo, illustrated boards, 2s.

Princess Olga.—Radna: A Novel. Crown 8vo, cloth extra, 6s.

Proctor (Richard A., B.A.), Works by.
Flowers of the Sky. With 55 Illustrations. Small crown 8vo, cloth extra, 3s. 6d.
Easy Star Lessons. With Star Maps for every Night in the Year. Crown 8vo, cloth, 6s.
Familiar Science Studies. Crown 8vo, cloth extra, 6s.
Saturn and its System. With 13 Steel Plates. Demy 8vo, cloth extra, 10s. 6d.
Mysteries of Time and Space. With numerous Illustrations. Crown 8vo, cloth extra, 6s.
The Universe of Suns, &c. With numerous Illustrations. Crown 8vo, cloth extra, 6s.
Wages and Wants of Science Workers. Crown 8vo, 1s. 6d.

Pryce (Richard).—Miss Maxwell's Affections. Crown 8vo, cloth,
with Frontispiece by HAL LUDLOW, 3s. 6d.; post 8vo, illustrated boards, 2s.

Rambosson (J.).—Popular Astronomy. Translated by C. B. PITMAN. With Coloured Frontispiece and numerous Illustrations. Crown 8vo, cloth extra, 7s. 6d.

Randolph (Lieut.-Col. George, U.S.A.).—Aunt Abigail Dykes:
A Novel. Crown 8vo, cloth extra, 7s. 6d.

Reade's (Charles) Novels.
Crown 8vo, cloth extra, mostly Illustrated, 3s. 6d. each; post 8vo, illustrated boards, 2s. each.
Peg Woffington. | Christie Johnstone. | Hard Cash. | Griffith Gaunt.
'It is Never Too Late to Mend.' | Foul Play. | Put Yourself in His Place.
The Course of True Love Never Did Run Smooth. | A Terrible Temptation.
The Autobiography of a Thief; Jack of all Trades; and James Lambert. | A Simpleton. | The Wandering Heir.
Love Me Little, Love Me Long. | A Woman-Hater.
The Double Marriage. | Singleheart and Doubleface.
The Cloister and the Hearth. | Good Stories of Men and other Animals.
| The Jilt, and other Stories.
| A Perilous Secret. | Readiana.

A New Collected LIBRARY EDITION, complete in Seventeen Volumes, set in new long primer type, printed on laid paper, and elegantly bound in cloth, price 3s. 6d. each, is now in course of publication. The volumes will appear in the following order:—

1. Peg Woffington; and Christie Johnstone.
2. Hard Cash.
3. The Cloister and the Hearth. With a Preface by Sir WALTER BESANT.
4. 'It is Never too Late to Mend.'
5. The Course of True Love Never Did Run Smooth; and Singleheart and Doubleface.
6. The Autobiography of a Thief; Jack of all Trades; A Hero and a Martyr; and The Wandering Heir.
7. Love Me Little, Love me Long.
8. The Double Marriage. [April.
9. Griffith Gaunt. [May.
10. Foul Play. [June.
11. Put Yourself in His Place. [July.
12. A Terrible Temptation. [August.
13. A Simpleton. [Sept.
14. A Woman-Hater. [Oct.
15. The Jilt, and other Stories; and Good Stories of Men & other Animals.[Nov.
16. A Perilous Secret. [Dec.
17. Readiana; & Bible Characters.[Jan.'97

POPULAR EDITIONS, medium 8vo, 6d. each: cloth, 1s. each.
'It is Never Too Late to Mend.' | The Cloister and the Hearth.
Peg Woffington; and Christie Johnstone.

'It is Never Too Late to Mend' and The Cloister and the Hearth in One Volume, medium 8vo, cloth, 2s.

Christie Johnstone. With Frontispiece. Choicely printed in Elzevir style. Fcap. 8vo, half-Roxb.2s.6d.
Peg Woffington. Choicely printed in Elzevir style. Fcap. 8vo, half-Roxburghe, 2s. 6d.
The Cloister and the Hearth. In Four Vols., post 8vo, with an Introduction by Sir WALTER BESANT, and a Frontispiece to each Vol., 14s. the set; and the ILLUSTRATED LIBRARY EDITION, with Illustrations on every page. Two Vols., crown 8vo, cloth gilt, 42s. net.
Bible Characters. Fcap. 8vo, leatherette, 1s.
Selections from the Works of Charles Reade. With an Introduction by Mrs. ALEX. IRELAND. Crown 8vo, buckram, with Portrait, 6s.; CHEAP EDITION, post 8vo, cloth limp, 2s. 6d.

Riddell (Mrs. J. H.), Novels by.
Weird Stories. Crown 8vo, cloth extra, 3s. 6d.; post 8vo, illustrated boards, 2s.
Post 8vo, illustrated boards, 2s. each.
The Uninhabited House. | Fairy Water.
The Prince of Wales's Garden Party. | Her Mother's Darling.
The Mystery in Palace Gardens. | The Nun's Curse. | Idle Tales.

Rimmer (Alfred), Works by. Square 8vo, cloth gilt, 7s. 6d. each.
Our Old Country Towns. With 55 Illustrations by the Author.
Rambles Round Eton and Harrow. With 50 Illustrations by the Author.
About England with Dickens. With 58 Illustrations by C. A. VANDERHOOF and A. RIMMER.

Rives (Amelie).—Barbara Dering. Crown 8vo, cloth extra, 3s. 6d.; post 8vo, illustrated boards, 2s.

Robinson Crusoe. By DANIEL DEFOE. With 37 Illustrations by GEORGE CRUIKSHANK. Post 8vo, half-cloth, 2s.; cloth extra, gilt edges, 2s. 6d.

Robinson (F. W.), Novels by.
Women are Strange. Post 8vo, illustrated boards, 2s.
The Hands of Justice. Crown 8vo, cloth extra, 3s. 6d.; post 8vo, illustrated boards, 2s.

The Woman in the Dark. Two Vols., 10s. net.

Robinson (Phil), Works by. Crown 8vo, cloth extra, 6s. each.
The Poets' Birds. | The Poets' Beasts.
The Poets and Nature: Reptiles, Fishes, and Insects.

Rochefoucauld's Maxims and Moral Reflections. With Notes and an Introductory Essay by SAINTE-BEUVE. Post 8vo, cloth limp, 2s.

Roll of Battle Abbey, The: A List of the Principal Warriors who came from Normandy with William the Conqueror, 1066. Printed in Gold and Colours, 5s.

Rosengarten (A.).—A Handbook of Architectural Styles. Translated by W. COLLETT-SANDARS. With 630 Illustrations. Crown 8vo, cloth extra, 7s. 6d.

Rowley (Hon. Hugh), Works by. Post 8vo, cloth, 2s. 6d. each.
Puniana: Riddles and Jokes. With numerous Illustrations.
More Puniana. Profusely Illustrated.

Runciman (James), Stories by. Post 8vo, bds., 2s. ea.; cl., 2s. 6d. ea.
Skippers and Shellbacks. | Grace Balmaign's Sweetheart.
Schools and Scholars.

Russell (Dora), Novels by. Crown 8vo, cloth, 3s. 6d. each.
A Country Sweetheart. | The Drift of Fate. [Shortly.

Russell (W. Clark), Books and Novels by.
Crown 8vo, cloth extra, 6s. each; post 8vo, illustrated boards, 2s. each; cloth limp, 2s. 6d. each.
Round the Galley-Fire. | A Book for the Hammock.
In the Middle Watch. | The Mystery of the 'Ocean Star.'
A Voyage to the Cape. | The Romance of Jenny Harlowe.

Crown 8vo, cloth extra, 3s. 6d. each; post 8vo, illustrated boards, 2s. each; cloth limp, 2s. 6d. each.
An Ocean Tragedy. | My Shipmate Louise. | Alone on a Wide Wide Sea.

Crown 8vo, cloth, 3s. 6d. each.
Is He the Man? | The Phantom Death, &c. With Frontispiece.
The Good Ship 'Mohock.' | The Convict Ship. [Shortly.

On the Fo'k'sle Head. Post 8vo, illustrated boards, 2s.; cloth limp, 2s. 6d.
Heart of Oak. Three Vols., crown 8vo, 15s. net.
The Tale of the Ten. Three Vols., crown 8vo, 15s. net.

Saint Aubyn (Alan), Novels by.
Crown 8vo, cloth extra, 3s. 6d. each; post 8vo, illustrated boards, 2s. each.
A Fellow of Trinity. With a Note by OLIVER WENDELL HOLMES and a Frontispiece.
The Junior Dean. | The Master of St. Benedict's. | To His Own Master.
Orchard Damerel.

Fcap. 8vo, cloth boards, 1s. 6d. each.
The Old Maid's Sweetheart. | Modest Little Sara.

Crown 8vo, cloth extra, 3s. 6d. each.
In the Face of the World. | The Tremlett Diamonds. [Shortly.

Sala (George A.).—Gaslight and Daylight. Post 8vo, boards, 2s.

Sanson. — Seven Generations of Executioners: Memoirs of the Sanson Family (1688 to 1847). Crown 8vo, cloth extra, 3s. 6d.

Saunders (John), Novels by.
Crown 8vo, cloth extra, 3s. 6d. each; post 8vo, illustrated boards, 2s. each.
Guy Waterman. | The Lion in the Path. | The Two Dreamers.

Bound to the Wheel. Crown 8vo, cloth extra, 3s. 6d.

Saunders (Katharine), Novels by.
Crown 8vo, cloth extra, 3s. 6d. each; post 8vo, illustrated boards, 2s. each.

Margaret and Elizabeth. | Heart Salvage.
The High Mills. | Sebastian.

Joan Merryweather. Post 8vo, illustrated boards, 2s.
Gideon's Rock. Crown 8vo, cloth extra, 3s. 6d.

Scotland Yard, Past and Present: Experiences of Thirty-seven Years. By Ex-Chief-Inspector CAVANAGH. Post 8vo, illustrated boards, 2s.; cloth, 2s. 6d.

Secret Out, The: One Thousand Tricks with Cards; with Entertaining Experiments in Drawing-room or 'White' Magic. By W. H. CREMER. With 300 Illustrations. Crown 8vo, cloth extra, 4s. 6d.

Seguin (L. G.), Works by.
The Country of the Passion Play (Oberammergau) and the Highlands of Bavaria. With Map and 37 Illustrations. Crown 8vo, cloth extra, 3s. 6d.
Walks in Algiers. With Two Maps and 16 Illustrations. Crown 8vo, cloth extra, 6s.

Senior (Wm.).—By Stream and Sea. Post 8vo, cloth, 2s. 6d.

Sergeant (Adeline).—Dr. Endicott's Experiment. Crown 8vo, buckram, 3s. 6d.

Shakespeare for Children: Lamb's Tales from Shakespeare. With Illustrations, coloured and plain, by J. MOYR SMITH. Crown 4to, cloth gilt, 3s. 6d.

Sharp (William).—Children of To-morrow. Crown 8vo, cloth, 6s.

Shelley's (Percy Bysshe) Complete Works in Verse and Prose. Edited, Prefaced, and Annotated by R. HERNE SHEPHERD. Five Vols., crown 8vo, cloth, 3s. 6d. each.
Poetical Works, in Three Vols.:
Vol. I. Introduction by the Editor; Posthumous Fragments of Margaret Nicholson; Shelley's Correspondence with Stockdale; The Wandering Jew; Queen Mab, with the Notes; Alastor, and other Poems; Rosalind and Helen; Prometheus Unbound; Adonais, &c.
,, II. Laon and Cythna; The Cenci; Julian and Maddalo; Swellfoot the Tyrant; The Witch of Atlas; Epipsychidion; Hellas.
,, III. Posthumous Poems; The Masque of Anarchy; and other Pieces.
Prose Works, in Two Vols.:
Vol. I. The Two Romances of Zastrozzi and St. Irvyne; the Dublin and Marlow Pamphlets; A Refutation of Deism; Letters to Leigh Hunt, and some Minor Writings and Fragments.
,, II. The Essays; Letters from Abroad; Translations and Fragments, edited by Mrs. SHELLEY. With a Biography of Shelley, and an Index of the Prose Works.
*** Also a few copies of a LARGE-PAPER EDITION, 5 vols., cloth, £2 12s. 6d.

Sherard (R. H.).—Rogues: A Novel. Crown 8vo, 1s.; cloth, 1s. 6d.

Sheridan (General P. H.), Personal Memoirs of. With Portraits, Maps, and Facsimiles. Two Vols., demy 8vo, cloth, 24s.

Sheridan's (Richard Brinsley) Complete Works, with Life and Anecdotes. Including his Dramatic Writings, his Works in Prose and Poetry, Translations, Speeches, and Jokes. With 10 Illustrations. Crown 8vo, half-bound, 7s. 6d.
The Rivals, The School for Scandal, and other Plays. Post 8vo, half-bound, 2s.
Sheridan's Comedies: The Rivals and The School for Scandal. Edited, with an Introduction and Notes to each Play, and a Biographical Sketch, by BRANDER MATTHEWS. With Illustrations. Demy 8vo, half-parchment, 12s. 6d.

Sidney's (Sir Philip) Complete Poetical Works, including all those in 'Arcadia.' With Portrait, Memorial-Introduction, Notes, &c., by the Rev. A. B. GROSART, D.D. Three Vols., crown 8vo, cloth boards, 18s.

Sims (George R.), Works by.
Post 8vo, illustrated boards, 2s. each; cloth limp, 2s. 6d. each.

Rogues and Vagabonds. | Tales of To-day.
The Ring o' Bells. | Dramas of Life. With 60 Illustrations.
Mary Jane's Memoirs. | Memoirs of a Landlady.
Mary Jane Married. | My Two Wives.
Tinkletop's Crime. | Scenes from the Show.
Zeph: A Circus Story, &c. | The Ten Commandments: Stories. [Shortly.

Crown 8vo, picture cover, 1s. each; cloth, 1s. 6d. each.
How the Poor Live; and Horrible London.
The Dagonet Reciter and Reader: Being Readings and Recitations in Prose and Verse, selected from his own Works by GEORGE R. SIMS.
The Case of George Candlemas. | Dagonet Ditties. (From *The Referee*.)

Dagonet Abroad. Crown 8vo, cloth, 3s. 6d.

Signboards: Their History, including Anecdotes of Famous Taverns and Remarkable Characters. By JACOB LARWOOD and JOHN CAMDEN HOTTEN. With Coloured Frontispiece and 94 Illustrations. Crown 8vo, cloth extra, 7s. 6d.

Sister Dora: A Biography. By MARGARET LONSDALE. With Four Illustrations. Demy 8vo, picture cover, 4d.; cloth, 6d.

Sketchley (Arthur).—A Match in the Dark. Post 8vo, boards, 2s.

Slang Dictionary (The): Etymological, Historical, and Anecdotal. Crown 8vo, cloth extra, 6s. 6d.

Smart (Hawley).—Without Love or Licence: A Novel. Crown 8vo, cloth extra, 3s. 6d.; post 8vo, illustrated boards, 2s.

Smith (J. Moyr), Works by.
The Prince of Argolis. With 130 Illustrations. Post 8vo, cloth extra, 3s. 6d.
The Wooing of the Water Witch. With numerous Illustrations. Post 8vo, cloth, 6s.

Society in London. Crown 8vo, 1s.; cloth, 1s. 6d.

Society in Paris: The Upper Ten Thousand. A Series of Letters from Count PAUL VASILI to a Young French Diplomat. Crown 8vo, cloth, 6s.

Somerset (Lord Henry).—Songs of Adieu. Small 4to, Jap. vel., 6s.

Spalding (T. A., LL.B.).— Elizabethan Demonology: An Essay on the Belief in the Existence of Devils. Crown 8vo, cloth extra, 5s.

Speight (T. W.), Novels by.
Post 8vo, illustrated boards, 2s. each.

The Mysteries of Heron Dyke.	Back to Life.
By Devious Ways, &c.	The Loudwater Tragedy.
Hoodwinked; & Sandycroft Mystery.	Burgo's Romance.
The Golden Hoop.	Quittance in Full.

Post 8vo, cloth limp, 1s. 6d. each.

A Barren Title.	Wife or No Wife?

Crown 8vo, cloth extra, 3s. 6d. each.

A Secret of the Sea.	The Grey Monk.

The Sandycroft Mystery. Crown 8vo, picture cover, 1s.
The Master of Trenance. Three Vols., crown 8vo, 15s. net.
A Husband from the Sea. Post 8vo, illustrated boards, 2s.

Spenser for Children. By M. H. TOWRY. With Coloured Illustrations by WALTER J. MORGAN. Crown 4to, cloth extra, 3s. 6d.

Stafford (John).—Doris and I, &c. Crown 8vo, cloth, 3s. 6d. [*Shortly.*

Starry Heavens (The): A POETICAL BIRTHDAY BOOK. Royal 16mo, cloth extra, 2s. 6d.

Stedman (E. C.), Works by. Crown 8vo, cloth extra, 9s. each.
Victorian Poets. | The Poets of America.

Stephens (Riccardo, M.B.).—The Cruciform Mark: The Strange Story of RICHARD TREGENNA, Bachelor of Medicine (Univ. Edinb.) Crown 8vo, cloth, 6s.

Sterndale (R. Armitage).—The Afghan Knife: A Novel. Crown 8vo, cloth extra, 3s. 6d.; post 8vo, illustrated boards, 2s.

Stevenson (R. Louis), Works by. Post 8vo, cloth limp, 2s. 6d. ea.
Travels with a Donkey. With a Frontispiece by WALTER CRANE.
An Inland Voyage. With a Frontispiece by WALTER CRANE.

Crown 8vo, buckram, gilt top, 6s. each.
Familiar Studies of Men and Books.
The Silverado Squatters. With Frontispiece by J. D. STRONG.
The Merry Men. | Underwoods: Poems.
Memories and Portraits.
Virginibus Puerisque, and other Papers. | Ballads. | Prince Otto.
Across the Plains, with other Memories and Essays.

New Arabian Nights. Crown 8vo, buckram, gilt top, 6s.; post 8vo, illustrated boards, 2s.
The Suicide Club; and The Rajah's Diamond. (From NEW ARABIAN NIGHTS.) With Eight Illustrations by W. J. HENNESSY. Crown 8vo, cloth, 5s.
The Edinburgh Edition of the Works of Robert Louis Stevenson. Twenty-seven Vols., demy 8vo. This Edition (which is limited to 1,000 copies) is sold only in Sets, the price of which may be learned from the Booksellers. The First Volume was published Nov., 1894.

Songs of Travel. Crown 8vo, buckram, 5s. [*Shortly.*
Weir of Hermiston. (R. L. STEVENSON'S LAST WORK.) Large crown 8vo, 6s. [*May.*

Stoddard (C. Warren).—Summer Cruising in the South Seas.
Illustrated by WALLIS MACKAY. Crown 8vo, cloth extra, 3s. 6d.

Stories from Foreign Novelists. With Notices by HELEN and ALICE ZIMMERN. Crown 8vo, cloth extra, 3s. 6d.; post 8vo, illustrated boards, 2s.

Strange Manuscript (A) Found in a Copper Cylinder. Crown 8vo, cloth extra, with 19 Illustrations by GILBERT GAUL, 5s.; post 8vo, illustrated boards, 2s.

Strange Secrets. Told by PERCY FITZGERALD, CONAN DOYLE, FLORENCE MARRYAT, &c. Post 8vo, illustrated boards, 2s.

Strutt (Joseph). — The Sports and Pastimes of the People of England; including the Rural and Domestic Recreations, May Games, Mummeries, Shows, &c., from the Earliest Period to the Present Time. Edited by WILLIAM HONE. With 140 Illustrations. Crown 8vo, cloth extra, 7s. 6d.

Swift's (Dean) Choice Works, in Prose and Verse. With Memoir, Portrait, and Facsimiles of the Maps in 'Gulliver's Travels.' Crown 8vo, cloth, 7s. 6d.
Gulliver's Travels, and **A Tale of a Tub.** Post 8vo, half-bound, 2s.
Jonathan Swift: A Study. By J. CHURTON COLLINS. Crown 8vo, cloth extra, 8s.

Swinburne (Algernon C.), Works by.

Selections from the Poetical Works of A. C. Swinburne. Fcap. 8vo, 6s.
Atalanta in Calydon. Crown 8vo, 6s.
Chastelard: A Tragedy. Crown 8vo, 7s.
Poems and Ballads. FIRST SERIES. Crown 8vo, or fcap. 8vo, 9s.
Poems and Ballads. SECOND SERIES. Crown 8vo, 9s.
Poems & Ballads. THIRD SERIES. Cr. 8vo, 7s.
Songs before Sunrise. Crown 8vo, 10s. 6d.
Bothwell: A Tragedy. Crown 8vo, 12s. 6d.
Songs of Two Nations. Crown 8vo, 6s.
George Chapman. (See Vol. II. of G. CHAPMAN'S Works.) Crown 8vo, 6s.
Essays and Studies. Crown 8vo, 12s.
Erechtheus: A Tragedy. Crown 8vo, 6s.

A Note on Charlotte Bronte. Cr. 8vo, 6s
A Study of Shakespeare. Crown 8vo, 8s.
Songs of the Springtides. Crown 8vo, 6s.
Studies in Song. Crown 8vo, 7s.
Mary Stuart: A Tragedy. Crown 8vo, 8s.
Tristram of Lyonesse. Crown 8vo, 9s.
A Century of Roundels. Small 4to, 8s.
A Midsummer Holiday. Crown 8vo, 7s.
Marino Faliero: A Tragedy. Crown 8vo, 6s.
A Study of Victor Hugo. Crown 8vo, 6s.
Miscellanies. Crown 8vo, 12s.
Locrine: A Tragedy. Crown 8vo, 6s.
A Study of Ben Jonson. Crown 8vo, 7s.
The Sisters: A Tragedy. Crown 8vo, 6s.
Astrophel, &c. Crown 8vo, 7s.
Studies in Prose and Poetry. Cr. 8vo, 9s.

Syntax's (Dr.) Three Tours: In Search of the Picturesque, in Search of Consolation, and in Search of a Wife. With ROWLANDSON'S Coloured Illustrations, and Life of the Author by J. C. HOTTEN. Crown 8vo, cloth extra, 7s. 6d.

Taine's History of English Literature. Translated by HENRY VAN LAUN. Four Vols., small demy 8vo, cloth boards, 30s.—POPULAR EDITION, Two Vols., large crown 8vo, cloth extra, 15s.

Taylor (Bayard). — Diversions of the Echo Club: Burlesques of Modern Writers. Post 8vo, cloth limp, 2s.

Taylor (Dr. J. E., F.L.S.), Works by. Crown 8vo, cloth, 5s. each.
The Sagacity and Morality of Plants: A Sketch of the Life and Conduct of the Vegetable Kingdom. With a Coloured Frontispiece and 100 Illustrations.
Our Common British Fossils, and Where to Find Them. With 331 Illustrations.
The Playtime Naturalist. With 366 Illustrations.

Taylor (Tom). — Historical Dramas. Containing 'Clancarty,' 'Jeanne Darc,' ''Twixt Axe and Crown,' 'The Fool's Revenge,' 'Arkwright's Wife, 'Anne Boleyn, 'Plot and Passion.' Crown 8vo, cloth extra, 7s. 6d.

* The Plays may also be had separately, at 1s. each.

Tennyson (Lord): A Biographical Sketch. By H. J. JENNINGS. Post 8vo, portrait cover, 1s.; cloth, 1s. 6d.

Thackerayana: Notes and Anecdotes. With Coloured Frontispiece and Hundreds of Sketches by WILLIAM MAKEPEACE THACKERAY. Crown 8vo, cloth extra, 7s. 6d.

Thames, A New Pictorial History of the. By A. S. KRAUSSE. With 340 Illustrations. Post 8vo, 1s.; cloth, 1s. 6d.

Thiers (Adolphe). — History of the Consulate and Empire of France under Napoleon. Translated by D. FORBES CAMPBELL and JOHN STEBBING. With 36 Steel Plates. 12 Vols., demy 8vo, cloth extra, 12s. each.

Thomas (Bertha), Novels by. Cr. 8vo, cl., 3s. 6d. ea.; post 8vo, 2s. ea.
The Violin-Player. | Proud Maisie.
Cressida. Post 8vo, illustrated boards, 2s.

Thomson's Seasons, and The Castle of Indolence. With Introduction by ALLAN CUNNINGHAM, and 48 Illustrations. Post 8vo, half-bound, 2s.

Thornbury (Walter), Books by.
The Life and Correspondence of J. M. W. Turner. With Illustrations in Colours. Crown 8vo, cloth extra, 7s. 6d.
Post 8vo, illustrated boards, 2s. each.
Old Stories Re-told. | Tales for the Marines.

Timbs (John), Works by. Crown 8vo, cloth extra, 7s. 6d. each.
The History of Clubs and Club Life in London: Anecdotes of its Famous Coffee-houses, Hostelries, and Taverns. With 42 Illustrations.
English Eccentrics and Eccentricities: Stories of Delusions, Impostures, Sporting Scenes, Eccentric Artists, Theatrical Folk, &c. With 48 Illustrations.

Transvaal (The). By JOHN DE VILLIERS. With Map. Crown 8vo, 1s.

Trollope (Anthony), Novels by.
Crown 8vo, cloth extra, 3s. 6d. each; post 8vo, illustrated boards, 2s. each.
The Way We Live Now. | Mr. Scarborough's Family.
Frau Frohmann. | The Land-Leaguers.
Post 8vo, illustrated boards, 2s. each.
Kept in the Dark. | The American Senator.
The Golden Lion of Granpere. | John Caldigate. | Marion Fay.

Trollope (Frances E.), Novels by.
Crown 8vo, cloth extra, 3s. 6d. each; post 8vo, illustrated boards, 2s. each.
Like Ships Upon the Sea. | Mabel's Progress. | Anne Furness.

Trollope (T. A.).—Diamond Cut Diamond. Post 8vo, illust. bds., 2s.

Trowbridge (J. T.).—Farnell's Folly. Post 8vo, illust. boards, 2s.

Tytler (C. C. Fraser-).—Mistress Judith: A Novel. Crown 8vo, cloth extra, 3s. 6d.; post 8vo, illustrated boards, 2s.

Tytler (Sarah), Novels by.
Crown 8vo, cloth extra, 3s. 6d. each; post 8vo, illustrated boards, 2s. each.
Lady Bell. | Buried Diamonds. | The Blackhall Ghosts.
Post 8vo, illustrated boards, 2s. each.
What She Came Through. | The Huguenot Family.
Citoyenne Jacqueline. | Noblesse Oblige.
The Bride's Pass. | Beauty and the Beast.
Saint Mungo's City. | Disappeared.
The Macdonald Lass. With Frontispiece. Crown 8vo, cloth, 3s. 6d.

Upward (Allen), Novels by.
The Queen Against Owen. Crown 8vo, cloth, with Frontispiece, 3s. 6d.; post 8vo, boards, 2s.
The Prince of Balkistan. Crown 8vo, cloth extra, 3s. 6d.
A Crown of Straw. Crown 8vo, cloth, 6s. [Shortly.

Vashti and Esther. By the Writer of 'Belle's' Letters in *The World*. Crown 8vo, cloth extra, 3s. 6d.

Villari (Linda).—A Double Bond: A Story. Fcap. 8vo, 1s.

Vizetelly (Ernest A.).—The Scorpion: A Romance of Spain. With a Frontispiece. Crown 8vo, cloth extra, 3s. 6d.

Walton and Cotton's Complete Angler; or, The Contemplative Man's Recreation, by IZAAK WALTON; and Instructions How to Angle, for a Trout or Grayling in a clear Stream, by CHARLES COTTON. With Memoirs and Notes by Sir HARRIS NICOLAS, and 61 Illustrations. Crown 8vo, cloth antique, 7s. 6d.

Walt Whitman, Poems by. Edited, with Introduction, by WILLIAM M. ROSSETTI. With Portrait. Crown 8vo, hand-made paper and buckram, 6s.

Ward (Herbert), Books by.
Five Years with the Congo Cannibals. With 92 Illustrations. Royal 8vo, cloth, 14s.
My Life with Stanley's Rear Guard. With Map. Post 8vo, 1s.; cloth, 1s. 6d.

Walford (Edward, M.A.), Works by.

Walford's County Families of the United Kingdom (1896). Containing the Descent, Birth, Marriage, Education, &c., of 12,000 Heads of Families, their Heirs, Offices, Addresses, Clubs, &c. Royal 8vo, cloth gilt, 50s.
Walford's Shilling Peerage (1896). Containing a List of the House of Lords, Scotch and Irish Peers, &c. 32mo, cloth, 1s.
Walford's Shilling Baronetage (1896). Containing a List of the Baronets of the United Kingdom, Biographical Notices, Addresses, &c. 32mo, cloth, 1s.
Walford's Shilling Knightage (1896). Containing a List of the Knights of the United Kingdom, Biographical Notices, Addresses, &c. 32mo, cloth, 1s.
Walford's Shilling House of Commons (1896). Containing a List of all the Members of the New Parliament, their Addresses, Clubs, &c. 32mo, cloth, 1s.
Walford's Complete Peerage, Baronetage, Knightage, and House of Commons (1896). Royal 32mo, cloth, gilt edges, 5s.

Tales of our Great Families. Crown 8vo, cloth extra, 3s. 6d.

Warner (Charles Dudley).—A Roundabout Journey. Crown 8vo, cloth extra, 6s.

Warrant to Execute Charles I. A Facsimile, with the 59 Signatures and Seals. Printed on paper 22 in. by 14 in. 2s.

Warrant to Execute Mary Queen of Scots. A Facsimile, including Queen Elizabeth's Signature and the Great Seal. 2s.

Washington's (George) Rules of Civility Traced to their Sources and Restored by MONCURE D. CONWAY. Fcap. 8vo, Japanese vellum, 2s. 6d.

Wassermann (Lillias), Novels by.

The Daffodils. Crown 8vo, 1s.; cloth, 1s. 6d.

The Marquis of Carabas. By AARON WATSON and LILLIAS WASSERMANN. Post 8vo, illustrated boards, 2s.

Weather, How to Foretell the, with the Pocket Spectroscope. By F. W. CORY. With Ten Illustrations. Crown 8vo, 1s.; cloth, 1s. 6d.

Webber (Byron).—Fun, Frolic, and Fancy. With 43 Illustrations by PHIL MAY and CHARLES MAY. Fcap. 4to, cloth, 5s.

Westall (William), Novels by.

Trust-Money. Post 8vo, illustrated boards, 2s.; cloth, 2s. 6d.
Sons of Belial. Two Vols., crown 8vo, 10s. net.

Westbury (Atha).—The Shadow of Hilton Fernbrook: A Romance of Maoriland. Crown 8vo, cloth, 3s. 6d. [Shortly.

Whist, How to Play Solo. By ABRAHAM S. WILKS and CHARLES F. PARDON. Post 8vo, cloth limp, 2s.

White (Gilbert).—The Natural History of Selborne. Post 8vo, printed on laid paper and half-bound, 2s.

Williams (W. Mattieu, F.R.A.S.), Works by.

Science in Short Chapters. Crown 8vo, cloth extra, 7s. 6d.
A Simple Treatise on Heat. With Illustrations. Crown 8vo, cloth, 2s. 6d.
The Chemistry of Cookery. Crown 8vo, cloth extra, 6s.
The Chemistry of Iron and Steel Making. Crown 8vo, cloth extra, 9s.
A Vindication of Phrenology. With Portrait and 43 Illusts. Demy 8vo, cloth extra, 12s. 6d.

Williamson (Mrs. F. H.).—A Child Widow. Post 8vo, bds., 2s.

Wills (W. H., M.D.).—An Easy-going Fellow. Crown 8vo, cloth, 6s. [Shortly.

Wilson (Dr. Andrew, F.R.S.E.), Works by.

Chapters on Evolution. With 259 Illustrations. Crown 8vo, cloth extra, 7s. 6d.
Leaves from a Naturalist's Note-Book. Post 8vo, cloth limp, 2s. 6d.
Leisure-Time Studies. With Illustrations. Crown 8vo, cloth extra, 6s.
Studies in Life and Sense. With numerous Illustrations. Crown 8vo, cloth extra, 6s.
Common Accidents: How to Treat Them. With Illustrations. Crown 8vo, 1s.; cloth, 1s. 6d.
Glimpses of Nature. With 35 Illustrations. Crown 8vo, cloth extra, 3s. 6d.

Winter (J. S.), Stories by. Post 8vo, illustrated boards, 2s. each; cloth limp, 2s. 6d. each.

Cavalry Life. | **Regimental Legends.**

A Soldier's Children. With 34 Illustrations by E. G. THOMSON and E. STUART HARDY. Crown 8vo, cloth extra, 3s. 6d.

Wissmann (Hermann von). — My Second Journey through Equatorial Africa. With 92 Illustrations. Demy 8vo, cloth, 16s.

Wood (H. F.), Detective Stories by. Post 8vo, boards, 2s. each.
The Passenger from Scotland Yard. | The Englishman of the Rue Cain.

Wood (Lady).—Sabina: A Novel. Post 8vo, illustrated boards, 2s.

Woolley (Celia Parker).—Rachel Armstrong; or, Love and Theology. Post 8vo, illustrated boards, 2s.; cloth, 2s. 6d.

Wright (Thomas), Works by. Crown 8vo, cloth extra, 7s. 6d. each.
The Caricature History of the Georges. With 400 Caricatures, Squibs, &c.
History of Caricature and of the Grotesque in Art, Literature, Sculpture, and Painting. Illustrated by F. W. FAIRHOLT, F.S.A.

Wynman (Margaret).—My Flirtations. With 13 Illustrations by J. BERNARD PARTRIDGE. Post 8vo, cloth, 3s. 6d.

Yates (Edmund), Novels by. Post 8vo, illustrated boards, 2s. each.
Land at Last. | The Forlorn Hope. | Castaway.

Zangwill (I.).—Ghetto Tragedies. With Three Illustrations by A. S. BOYD. Fcap. 8vo, picture cover, 1s. net.

Zola (Emile), Novels by. Crown 8vo, cloth extra, 3s. 6d. each.
The Fat and the Thin. Translated by ERNEST A. VIZETELLY.
Money. Translated by ERNEST A. VIZETELLY.
The Downfall. Translated by E. A. VIZETELLY.
The Dream. Translated by ELIZA CHASE. With Eight Illustrations by JEANNIOT.
Doctor Pascal. Translated by E. A. VIZETELLY. With Portrait of the Author.
Lourdes. Translated by ERNEST A. VIZETELLY.
Rome. Translated by ERNEST A. VIZETELLY. [Shortly.

SOME BOOKS CLASSIFIED IN SERIES.

⁎ *For fuller cataloguing, see alphabetical arrangement, pp. 1-26.*

The Mayfair Library. Post 8vo, cloth limp, 2s. 6d. per Volume.

A Journey Round My Room. By X. DE MAISTRE. Translated by Sir HENRY ATTWELL.
Quips and Quiddities. By W. D. ADAMS.
The Agony Column of 'The Times.'
Melancholy Anatomised; Abridgment of BURTON.
Poetical Ingenuities. By W. T. DOBSON.
The Cupboard Papers. By FIN-BEC.
W. S. Gilbert's Plays. Three Series.
Songs of Irish Wit and Humour.
Animals and their Masters. By Sir A. HELPS.
Social Pressure. By Sir A. HELPS.
Curiosities of Criticism. By H. J. JENNINGS.
The Autocrat of the Breakfast-Table. By OLIVER WENDELL HOLMES.
Pencil and Palette. By R. KEMPT.
Little Essays: from LAMB'S LETTERS.
Forensic Anecdotes. By JACOB LARWOOD.
Theatrical Anecdotes. By JACOB LARWOOD.
Jeux d'Esprit. Edited by HENRY S. LEIGH.
Witch Stories. By E. LYNN LINTON.
Ourselves. By E. LYNN LINTON.
Pastimes and Players. By R. MACGREGOR.
New Paul and Virginia. By W. H. MALLOCK.
The New Republic. By W. H. MALLOCK.
Puck on Pegasus. By H. C. PENNELL.
Pegasus Re-saddled. By H. C. PENNELL.
Muses of Mayfair. Edited by H. C. PENNELL.
Thoreau: His Life and Aims. By H. A. PAGE.
Punians. By Hon. HUGH ROWLEY.
More Punians. By Hon. HUGH ROWLEY.
The Philosophy of Handwriting.
By Stream and Sea. By WILLIAM SENIOR.
Leaves from a Naturalist's Note-Book. By Dr. ANDREW WILSON.

The Golden Library. Post 8vo, cloth limp, 2s. per Volume.

Diversions of the Echo Club. BAYARD TAYLOR.
Songs for Sailors. By W. C. BENNETT.
Lives of the Necromancers. By W. GODWIN.
The Poetical Works of Alexander Pope.
Scenes of Country Life. By EDWARD JESSE.
Tale for a Chimney Corner. By LEIGH HUNT.
The Autocrat of the Breakfast Table. By OLIVER WENDELL HOLMES.
La Mort d'Arthur: Selections from MALLORY.
Provincial Letters of Blaise Pascal.
Maxims and Reflections of Rochefoucauld.

The Wanderer's Library. Crown 8vo, cloth extra, 3s. 6d. each.

Wanderings in Patagonia. By JULIUS BEERBOHM. Illustrated.
Merrie England in the Olden Time. By G. DANIEL. Illustrated by ROBERT CRUIKSHANK.
Circus Life. By THOMAS FROST.
Lives of the Conjurers. By THOMAS FROST.
The Old Showmen and the Old London Fairs. By THOMAS FROST.
Low-Life Deeps. By JAMES GREENWOOD.
The Wilds of London. By JAMES GREENWOOD.
Tunis. By Chev. HESSE-WARTEGG. 22 Illusts.
Life and Adventures of a Cheap Jack.
World Behind the Scenes. By P. FITZGERALD.
Tavern Anecdotes and Sayings.
The Genial Showman. By E. P. HINGSTON.
Story of London Parks. By JACOB LARWOOD.
London Characters. By HENRY MAYHEW.
Seven Generations of Executioners.
Summer Cruising in the South Seas. By C. WARREN STODDARD. Illustrated.

CHATTO & WINDUS, PUBLISHERS, PICCADILLY.   27

BOOKS IN SERIES—*continued*.

Handy Novels. Fcap. 8vo, cloth boards, 1s. 6d. each.

The Old Maid's Sweetheart. By A. ST. AUBYN.
Modest Little Sara. By ALAN ST. AUBYN.
Seven Sleepers of Ephesus. M. E. COLERIDGE.
Taken from the Enemy. By H. NEWBOLT.
A Lost Soul. By W. L. ALDEN.
Dr. Palliser's Patient. By GRANT ALLEN.
Monte Carlo Stories. By JOAN BARRETT.
Black Spirits and White. By R. A. CRAM.

My Library. Printed on laid paper, post 8vo, half-Roxburghe, 2s. 6d. each.

Citation and Examination of William Shakspeare. By W. S. LANDOR.
The Journal of Maurice de Guerin.
Christie Johnstone. By CHARLES READE.
Peg Woffington. By CHARLES READE.
The Dramatic Essays of Charles Lamb.

The Pocket Library. Post 8vo, printed on laid paper and hf.-bd., 2s. each.

The Essays of Elia. By CHARLES LAMB.
Robinson Crusoe. Illustrated by G. CRUIKSHANK.
Whims and Oddities. By THOMAS HOOD.
The Barber's Chair. By DOUGLAS JERROLD.
Gastronomy. By BRILLAT-SAVARIN.
The Epicurean, &c. By THOMAS MOORE.
Leigh Hunt's Essays. Edited by E. OLLIER.
White's Natural History of Selborne.
Gulliver's Travels, &c. By Dean SWIFT.
Plays by RICHARD BRINSLEY SHERIDAN.
Anecdotes of the Clergy. By JACOB LARWOOD.
Thomson's Seasons. Illustrated.
Autocrat of the Breakfast-Table and The Professor at the Breakfast-Table. By O. W. HOLMES.

THE PICCADILLY NOVELS.
LIBRARY EDITIONS OF NOVELS, many Illustrated, crown 8vo, cloth extra, 3s. 6d. each.

By F. M. ALLEN.
Green as Grass.

By GRANT ALLEN.
Philistia.
Strange Stories.
Babylon.
For Maimie's Sake.
In all Shades.
The Beckoning Hand.
The Devil's Die.
This Mortal Coil.
The Tents of Shem.
The Great Taboo.
Dumaresq's Daughter.
Duchess of Powysland.
Blood Royal.
Ivan Greet's Masterpiece.
The Scallywag.
At Market Value.
Under Sealed Orders.

By MARY ANDERSON.
Othello's Occupation.

By EDWIN L. ARNOLD.
Phra the Phœnician. | Constable of St. Nicholas.

By ROBERT BARR.
In a Steamer Chair. | From Whose Bourne.

By FRANK BARRETT.
The Woman of the Iron Bracelets.

By 'BELLE.'
Vashti and Esther.

By Sir W. BESANT and J. RICE.
Ready-Money Mortiboy.
My Little Girl.
With Harp and Crown.
This Son of Vulcan.
The Golden Butterfly.
The Monks of Thelema.
By Celia's Arbour.
Chaplain of the Fleet.
The Seamy Side.
The Case of Mr. Lucraft.
In Trafalgar's Bay.
The Ten Years' Tenant.

By Sir WALTER BESANT.
All Sorts and Conditions of Men.
The Captains' Room.
All in a Garden Fair.
Dorothy Forster.
Uncle Jack.
The World Went Very Well Then.
Children of Gibeon.
Herr Paulus.
For Faith and Freedom.
To Call Her Mine.
The Bell of St. Paul's.
The Holy Rose.
Armorel of Lyonesse.
S. Katherine's by Tower.
Verbena Camellia Stephanotis.
The Ivory Gate.
The Rebel Queen.
Beyond the Dreams of Avarice.

By PAUL BOURGET.
A Living Lie.

By ROBERT BUCHANAN.
Shadow of the Sword.
A Child of Nature.
God and the Man.
Martyrdom of Madeline
Love Me for Ever.
Annan Water.
Foxglove Manor.
The New Abelard.
Matt. | Rachel Dene.
Master of the Mine.
The Heir of Linne.
Woman and the Man.
Red and White Heather.

ROB. BUCHANAN & HY. MURRAY.
The Charlatan.

By J. MITCHELL CHAPPLE.
The Minor Chord.

By HALL CAINE.
The Shadow of a Crime. | The Deemster.
A Son of Hagar.

By MACLAREN COBBAN.
The Red Sultan. | The Burden of Isabel.

By MORT. & FRANCES COLLINS.
Transmigration.
Blacksmith & Scholar.
The Village Comedy.
From Midnight to Midnight.
You Play me False.

By WILKIE COLLINS.
Armadale. | AfterDark.
No Name.
Antonina.
Basil.
Hide and Seek.
The Dead Secret.
Queen of Hearts.
My Miscellanies.
The Woman in White.
The Moonstone.
Man and Wife.
Poor Miss Finch.
Miss or Mrs. ?
The New Magdalen.
The Frozen Deep.
The Two Destinies.
The Law and the Lady.
The Haunted Hotel.
The Fallen Leaves.
Jezebel's Daughter.
The Black Robe.
Heart and Science.
'I Say No.'
Little Novels.
The Evil Genius.
The Legacy of Cain.
A Rogue's Life.
Blind Love.

By DUTTON COOK.
Paul Foster's Daughter.

By E. H. COOPER.
Geoffory Hamilton.

By V. CECIL COTES.
Two Girls on a Barge.

By C. EGBERT CRADDOCK.
His Vanished Star.

By H. N. CRELLIN.
Romances of the Old Seraglio.

By MATT CRIM.
The Adventures of a Fair Rebel.

By S. R. CROCKETT and others.
Tales of Our Coast.

By B. M. CROKER.
Diana Barrington.
Proper Pride.
A Family Likeness.
Pretty Miss Neville.
A Bird of Passage.
'To Let.'
Mr. Jervis.
Village Tales & Jungle Tragedies.
The Real Lady Hilda.

By WILLIAM CYPLES.
Hearts of Gold.

By ALPHONSE DAUDET.
The Evangelist ; or, Port Salvation.

By H. COLEMAN DAVIDSON.
Mr. Sadler's Daughters.

By ERASMUS DAWSON.
The Fountain of Youth.

By JAMES DE MILLE.
A Castle in Spain.

CHATTO & WINDUS, PUBLISHERS, PICCADILLY.

The Piccadilly (3/6) Novels—*continued*.

By J. LEITH DERWENT.
Our Lady of Tears. | Circe's Lovers.

By DICK DONOVAN.
Tracked to Doom. | The Mystery of Jamaica
Man from Manchester. | Terrace.

By A. CONAN DOYLE.
The Firm of Girdlestone.

By S. JEANNETTE DUNCAN.
A Daughter of To-day. | Vernon's Aunt.

By G. MANVILLE FENN.
The New Mistress. | The Tiger Lily.
Witness to the Deed. | The White Virgin.

By PERCY FITZGERALD.
Fatal Zero.

By R. E. FRANCILLON.
One by One. | Ropes of Sand.
A Dog and his Shadow. | Jack Doyle's Daughter.
A Real Queen. |

Prefaced by **Sir BARTLE FRERE.**
Pandurang Hari.

BY EDWARD GARRETT.
The Capel Girls.

By PAUL GAULOT.
The Red Shirts.

By CHARLES GIBBON.
Robin Gray. | The Golden Shaft.
Loving a Dream. |

By E. GLANVILLE.
The Lost Heiress. | The Fossicker.
A Fair Colonist. | The Golden Rock.

By E. J. GOODMAN.
The Fate of Herbert Wayne.

By Rev. S. BARING GOULD.
Red Spider. | Eve.

By CECIL GRIFFITH.
Corinthia Marazion.

By SYDNEY GRUNDY.
The Days of his Vanity.

By THOMAS HARDY.
Under the Greenwood Tree.

By BRET HARTE.
A Waif of the Plains. | Susy.
A Ward of the Golden | Sally Dows.
  Gate. | A Protégée of Jack
A Sappho of Green | Hamlin's.
  Springs. | Bell-Ringer of Angel's.
Col. Starbottle's Client. | Clarence.

By JULIAN HAWTHORNE.
Garth. | Beatrix Randolph.
Ellice Quentin. | David Poindexter's Dis-
Sebastian Strome. | appearance.
Dust. | The Spectre of the
Fortune's Fool. | Camera.

By Sir A. HELPS.
Ivan de Biron.

By I. HENDERSON.
Agatha Page.

By G. A. HENTY.
Rujub the Juggler. | Dorothy's Double.

By JOHN HILL.
The Common Ancestor.

By Mrs. HUNGERFORD.
Lady Verner's Flight. | The Three Graces.
The Red-House Mystery. |

By Mrs. ALFRED HUNT.
The Leaden Casket. | Self-Condemned.
That Other Person. | Mrs. Juliet.

By C. J. CUTCLIFFE HYNE.
Honour of Thieves.

By R. ASHE KING.
A Drawn Game.
'The Wearing of the Green.

By EDMOND LEPELLETIER.
Madame Sans-Gêne.

By HARRY LINDSAY.
Rhoda Roberts.

By E. LYNN LINTON.
Patricia Kemball. | Sowing the Wind.
Under which Lord? | The Atonement of Leam
'My Love!' | Dundas.
Ione. | The World Well Lost.
Paston Carew. | The One Too Many.

By HENRY W. LUCY.
Gideon Fleyce.

By JUSTIN McCARTHY.
A Fair Saxon. | Miss Misanthrope.
Linley Rochford. | Donna Quixote.
Dear Lady Disdain. | Red Diamonds.
Camiola. | Maid of Athens.
Waterdale Neighbours. | The Dictator.
My Enemy's Daughter. | The Comet of a Season.

By JUSTIN H. McCARTHY.
A London Legend.

By GEORGE MACDONALD.
Heather and Snow. | Phantastes.

By L. T. MEADE.
A Soldier of Fortune. | In an Iron Grip.

By BERTRAM MITFORD.
The Gun-Runner. | The King's Assegai.
The Luck of Gerard | Renshaw Fanning's
  Ridgeley. | Quest.

By J. E. MUDDOCK.
Maid Marian and Robin Hood.
Basile the Jester.

By D. CHRISTIE MURRAY.
A Life's Atonement. | First Person Singular.
Joseph's Coat. | Cynic Fortune.
Coals of Fire. | The Way of the World.
Old Blazer's Hero. | BobMartin's Little Girl.
Val Strange. | Hearts. | Time's Revenges.
A Model Father. | A Wasted Crime.
By the Gate of the Sea. | In Direst Peril.
A Bit of Human Nature. | Mount Despair.

By MURRAY and HERMAN.
The Bishops' Bible. | Paul Jones's Alias.
One Traveller Returns. |

By HUME NISBET.
'Bail Up!'

By W. E. NORRIS.
Saint Ann's. | Billy Bellew.

By G. OHNET.
A Weird Gift.

By OUIDA.
Held in Bondage. | Two Little Wooden
Strathmore. | Shoes.
Chandos. | In a Winter City.
Under Two Flags. | Friendship.
Idalia. | Moths.
Cecil Castlemaine's | Ruffino.
  Gage. | Pipistrello.
Tricotrin. | A Village Commune.
Puck. | Bimbi.
Folle Farine. | Wanda.
A Dog of Flanders. | Frescoes. | Othmar.
Pascarel. | In Maremma.
Signa. | Syrlin. | Guilderoy.
Princess Napraxine. | Santa Barbara.
Ariadne. | Two Offenders.

By MARGARET A. PAUL.
Gentle and Simple.

By JAMES PAYN.
Lost Sir Massingberd. | High Spirits.
Less Black than We're | Under One Roof.
  Painted. | Glow-worm Tales.
A Confidential Agent. | The Talk of the Town.
A Grape from a Thorn. | Holiday Tasks.
In Peril and Privation. | For Cash Only.
The Mystery of Mir- | The Burnt Million.
  By Proxy. [bridge. | The Word and the Will.
The Canon's Ward. | Sunny Stories.
Walter's Word. | A Trying Patient.

THE PICCADILLY (3/6) NOVELS—*continued*.

By Mrs. CAMPBELL PRAED.
Outlaw and Lawmaker. | Christina Chard.

By E. C. PRICE.
Valentina. | Mrs. Lancaster's Rival.
The Foreigners.

By RICHARD PRYCE.
Miss Maxwell's Affections.

By CHARLES READE.
It is Never Too Late to Mend. | Singleheart and Doubleface.
The Double Marriage. | Good Stories of Men and other Animals.
Love Me Little, Love Me Long. | Hard Cash.
The Cloister and the Hearth. | Peg Woffington.
The Course of True Love. | Christie Johnstone.
The Autobiography of a Thief. | Griffith Gaunt.
Put Yourself in His Place. | Foul Play.
A Terrible Temptation. | The Wandering Heir.
The Jilt. | A Woman-Hater.
 | A Simpleton.
 | A Perilous Secret.
 | Readiana.

By Mrs. J. H. RIDDELL.
Weird Stories.

By AMELIE RIVES.
Barbara Dering.

By F. W. ROBINSON.
The Hands of Justice.

By DORA RUSSELL.
A Country Sweetheart. | The Drift of Fate.

By W. CLARK RUSSELL.
Ocean Tragedy. | Is He the Man?
My Shipmate Louise. | The Good Ship 'Mohock.'
Alone on Wide Wide Sea |
The Phantom Death. | The Convict Ship.

By JOHN SAUNDERS.
Guy Waterman. | The Two Dreamers.
Bound to the Wheel. | The Lion in the Path.

By KATHARINE SAUNDERS.
Margaret and Elizabeth | Heart Salvage.
Gideon's Rock. | Sebastian.
The High Mills.

By ADELINE SERGEANT.
Dr. Endicott's Experiment.

By HAWLEY SMART.
Without Love or Licence.

By T. W. SPEIGHT.
A Secret of the Sea. | The Grey Monk.

By ALAN ST. AUBYN.
A Fellow of Trinity. | In Face of the World.
The Junior Dean. | Orchard Damerel.
Master of St. Benedict's. | The Tremlett Diamonds.
To his Own Master.

By JOHN STAFFORD.
Doris and I.

By R. A. STERNDALE.
The Afghan Knife.

By BERTHA THOMAS.
Proud Maisie. | The Violin-Player.

By ANTHONY TROLLOPE.
The Way we Live Now. | Scarborough's Family.
Frau Frohmann. | The Land-Leaguers.

By FRANCES E. TROLLOPE.
Like Ships upon the Sea. | Anne Furness.
 | Mabel's Progress.

By IVAN TURGENIEFF, &c.
Stories from Foreign Novelists.

By MARK TWAIN.
The American Claimant. | Pudd'nhead Wilson.
The £1,000,000 Bank-note. | Tom Sawyer, Detective.
Tom Sawyer Abroad.

By C. C. FRASER-TYTLER.
Mistress Judith.

By SARAH TYTLER.
Lady Bell. | The Blackhall Ghosts.
Buried Diamonds. | The Macdonald Lass.

By ALLEN UPWARD.
The Queen against Owen.
The Prince of Balkistan.

By E. A. VIZETELLY.
The Scorpion: A Romance of Spain.

By ATHA WESTBURY.
The Shadow of Hilton Fernbrook.

By JOHN STRANGE WINTER.
A Soldier's Children.

By MARGARET WYNMAN.
My Flirtations.

By E. ZOLA.
The Downfall. | Money. | Lourdes.
The Dream. | The Fat and the Thin.
Dr. Pascal. | Rome.

CHEAP EDITIONS OF POPULAR NOVELS.
Post 8vo, illustrated boards, 2s. each.

By ARTEMUS WARD.
Artemus Ward Complete.

By EDMOND ABOUT.
The Fellah.

By HAMILTON AÏDÉ.
Carr of Carrlyon. | Confidences.

By MARY ALBERT.
Brooke Finchley's Daughter.

By Mrs. ALEXANDER.
Maid, Wife or Widow? | Valerie's Fate.

By GRANT ALLEN.
Philistia. | The Great Taboo.
Strange Stories. | Dumaresq's Daughter.
Babylon | Duchess of Powysland.
For Maimie's Sake. | Blood Royal.
In all Shades. | Ivan Greet's Masterpiece.
The Beckoning Hand. |
The Devil's Die. | The Scallywag.
The Tents of Shem. | This Mortal Coil.

By E. LESTER ARNOLD.
Phra the Phœnician.

By SHELSLEY BEAUCHAMP.
Grantley Grange.

BY FRANK BARRETT.
Fettered for Life. | A Prodigal's Progress.
Little Lady Linton. | Found Guilty.
Between Life & Death. | A Recoiling Vengeance.
The Sin of Olga Zassoulich. | For Love and Honour.
 | John Ford; and His Helpmate.
Folly Morrison. |
Lieut. Barnabas. | The Woman of the Iron Bracelets.
Honest Davie. |

By Sir W. BESANT and J. RICE.
Ready-Money Mortiboy | By Celia's Arbour.
My Little Girl. | Chaplain of the Fleet.
With Harp and Crown. | The Seamy Side.
This Son of Vulcan. | The Case of Mr. Lucraft.
The Golden Butterfly. | In Trafalgar's Bay.
The Monks of Thelema. | The Ten Years' Tenant.

By Sir WALTER BESANT.
All Sorts and Conditions of Men. | For Faith and Freedom.
 | To Call Her Mine.
The Captains' Room. | The Bell of St. Paul's.
All in a Garden Fair. | The Holy Rose.
Dorothy Forster. | Armorel of Lyonesse.
Uncle Jack. | S. Katherine's by Tower.
The World Went Very Well Then. | Verbena Camellia Stephanotis.
Children of Gibeon. | The Ivory Gate.
Herr Paulus. | The Rebel Queen.

By AMBROSE BIERCE.
In the Midst of Life.

Two-Shilling Novels—*continued.*

By FREDERICK BOYLE.
Camp Notes. | Chronicles of No-man's
Savage Life. | Land.

BY BRET HARTE.
Californian Stories. | Flip. | Maruja.
Gabriel Conroy. | A Phyllis of the Sierras.
The Luck of Roaring | A Waif of the Plains.
Camp. | A Ward of the Golden
An Heiress of Red Dog. | Gate.

By HAROLD BRYDGES.
Uncle Sam at Home.

By ROBERT BUCHANAN.
Shadow of the Sword. | The Martyrdom of Ma-
A Child of Nature. | deline.
God and the Man. | The New Abelard.
Love Me for Ever. | Matt.
Foxglove Manor. | The Heir of Linne.
The Master of the Mine. | Woman and the Man.
Annan Water.

By HALL CAINE.
The Shadow of a Crime. | The Deemster.
A Son of Hagar.

By Commander CAMERON.
The Cruise of the 'Black Prince.'

By Mrs. LOVETT CAMERON.
Deceivers Ever. | Juliet's Guardian.

By HAYDEN CARRUTH.
The Adventures of Jones.

By AUSTIN CLARE.
For the Love of a Lass.

By Mrs. ARCHER CLIVE.
Paul Ferroll.
Why Paul Ferroll Killed his Wife.

By MACLAREN COBBAN.
The Cure of Souls. | The Red Sultan.

By C. ALLSTON COLLINS.
The Bar Sinister.

By MORT. & FRANCES COLLINS.
Sweet Anne Page. | Sweet and Twenty.
Transmigration. | The Village Comedy.
From Midnight to Mid- | You Play me False.
night. | Blacksmith and Scholar
A Fight with Fortune. | Frances.

By WILKIE COLLINS.
Armadale. | AfterDark. | My Miscellanies.
No Name. | The Woman in White.
Antonina. | The Moonstone.
Basil. | Man and Wife.
Hide and Seek. | Poor Miss Finch.
The Dead Secret. | The Fallen Leaves.
Queen of Hearts. | Jezebel's Daughter.
Miss or Mrs.? | The Black Robe.
The New Magdalen. | Heart and Science.
The Frozen Deep. | 'I Say No!'
The Law and the Lady | The Evil Genius.
The Two Destinies. | Little Novels.
The Haunted Hotel. | Legacy of Cain.
A Rogue's Life. | Blind Love.

By M. J. COLQUHOUN.
Every Inch a Soldier.

By DUTTON COOK.
Leo. | Paul Foster's Daughter.

By C. EGBERT CRADDOCK.
The Prophet of the Great Smoky Mountains.

By MATT CRIM.
The Adventures of a Fair Rebel.

By B. M. CROKER.
Pretty Miss Neville. | Proper Pride.
Diana Barrington. | A Family Likeness.
'To Let.' | Village Tales and Jungle
A Bird of Passage. | Tragedies.

By W. CYPLES.
Hearts of Gold.

By ALPHONSE DAUDET.
The Evangelist; or, Port Salvation.

By ERASMUS DAWSON.
The Fountain of Youth.

By JAMES DE MILLE.
A Castle in Spain.

By J. LEITH DERWENT.
Our Lady of Tears. | Circe's Lovers.

By CHARLES DICKENS.
Sketches by Boz. | Nicholas Nickleby.
Oliver Twist.

By DICK DONOVAN.
The Man-Hunter. | In the Grip of the Law.
Tracked and Taken. | From Information Re-
Caught at Last! | ceived.
Wanted! | Tracked to Doom.
Who Poisoned Hetty | Link by Link
Duncan? | Suspicion Aroused.
Man from Manchester. | Dark Deeds.
A Detective's Triumphs | Riddles Read.

By Mrs. ANNIE EDWARDES.
A Point of Honour. | Archie Lovell.

By M. BETHAM-EDWARDS.
Felicia. | Kitty.

By EDWARD EGGLESTON.
Roxy.

By G. MANVILLE FENN.
The New Mistress. | The Tiger Lily.
Witness to the Deed.

By PERCY FITZGERALD.
Bella Donna. | Second Mrs. Tillotson.
Never Forgotten. | Seventy-five Brooke
Polly. | Street.
Fatal Zero. | The Lady of Brantome.

By P. FITZGERALD and others.
Strange Secrets.

By ALBANY DE FONBLANQUE.
Filthy Lucre.

By R. E. FRANCILLON.
Olympia. | King or Knave?
One by One. | Romances of the Law.
A Real Queen. | Ropes of Sand.
Queen Cophetua. | A Dog and his Shadow.

By HAROLD FREDERIC.
Seth's Brother's Wife. | The Lawton Girl.

Prefaced by Sir BARTLE FRERE.
Pandurang Hari.

By HAIN FRISWELL.
One of Two.

By EDWARD GARRETT.
The Capel Girls.

By GILBERT GAUL.
A Strange Manuscript.

By CHARLES GIBBON.
Robin Gray. | In Honour Bound.
Fancy Free. | Flower of the Forest.
For Lack of Gold. | The Braes of Yarrow.
What will World Say? | The Golden Shaft.
In Love and War. | Of High Degree.
For the King. | By Mead and Stream.
In Pastures Green. | Loving a Dream.
Queen of the Meadow. | A Hard Knot.
A Heart's Problem. | Heart's Delight.
The Dead Heart. | Blood-Money.

By WILLIAM GILBERT.
Dr. Austin's Guests. | The Wizard of the
James Duke. | Mountain.

By ERNEST GLANVILLE.
The Lost Heiress. | The Fossicker.
A Fair Colonist.

By Rev. S. BARING GOULD.
Red Spider. | Eve.

By HENRY GREVILLE.
A Noble Woman. | Nikanor.

By CECIL GRIFFITH.
Corinthia Marazion.

By SYDNEY GRUNDY.
The Days of his Vanity.

By JOHN HABBERTON.
Brueton's Bayou. | Country Luck.

By ANDREW HALLIDAY.
Every-day Papers.

By Lady DUFFUS HARDY.
Paul Wynter's Sacrifice.

TWO-SHILLING NOVELS—*continued.*

By THOMAS HARDY.
Under the Greenwood Tree.

By J. BERWICK HARWOOD.
The Tenth Earl.

By JULIAN HAWTHORNE.
Garth.
Ellice Quentin.
Fortune's Fool.
Miss Cadogna.
Sebastian Strome.
Dust.
Beatrix Randolph.
Love—or a Name.
David Poindexter's Disappearance.
The Spectre of the Camera.

By Sir ARTHUR HELPS.
Ivan de Biron.

By G. A. HENTY.
Rujub the Juggler.

By HENRY HERMAN.
A Leading Lady.

By HEADON HILL.
Zambra the Detective.

By JOHN HILL.
Treason Felony.

By Mrs. CASHEL HOEY.
The Lover's Creed.

By Mrs. GEORGE HOOPER.
The House of Raby.

By TIGHE HOPKINS.
Twixt Love and Duty.

By Mrs. HUNGERFORD.
A Maiden all Forlorn.
In Durance Vile.
Marvel.
A Mental Struggle.
A Modern Circe.
Lady Verner's Flight.
The Red House Mystery.

By Mrs. ALFRED HUNT.
Thornicroft's Model.
That Other Person.
Self-Condemned.
The Leaden Casket.

By JEAN INGELOW.
Fated to be Free.

By WM. JAMESON.
My Dead Self.

By HARRIETT JAY.
The Dark Colleen. | Queen of Connaught.

By MARK KERSHAW.
Colonial Facts and Fictions.

By R. ASHE KING.
A Drawn Game.
'The Wearing of the Green.'
Passion's Slave.
Bell Barry.

By JOHN LEYS.
The Lindsays.

By E. LYNN LINTON.
Patricia Kemball.
The World Well Lost.
Under which Lord?
Paston Carew.
'My Love!'
Ione.
The Atonement of Leam Dundas.
With a Silken Thread.
Rebel of the Family.
Sowing the Wind.
The One Too Many.

By HENRY W. LUCY.
Gideon Fleyce.

By JUSTIN McCARTHY.
Dear Lady Disdain.
Waterdale Neighbours.
My Enemy's Daughter.
A Fair Saxon.
Linley Rochford.
Miss Misanthrope.
Camiola.
Donna Quixote.
Maid of Athens.
The Comet of a Season.
The Dictator.
Red Diamonds.

By HUGH MACCOLL.
Mr. Stranger's Sealed Packet.

By GEORGE MACDONALD.
Heather and Snow.

By AGNES MACDONELL.
Quaker Cousins.

By KATHARINE S. MACQUOID.
The Evil Eye. | Lost Rose.

By W. H. MALLOCK.
A Romance of the Nineteenth Century.
The New Republic.

By FLORENCE MARRYAT.
Open ! Sesame !
Fighting the Air.
A Harvest of Wild Oats.
Written in Fire.

By J. MASTERMAN.
Half-a-dozen Daughters.

By BRANDER MATTHEWS.
A Secret of the Sea.

By L. T. MEADE.
A Soldier of Fortune.

By LEONARD MERRICK.
The Man who was Good.

By JEAN MIDDLEMASS.
Touch and Go. | Mr. Dorillion.

By Mrs. MOLESWORTH.
Hathercourt Rectory.

By J. E. MUDDOCK.
Stories Weird and Wonderful.
The Dead Man's Secret.
From the Bosom of the Deep.

By D. CHRISTIE MURRAY.
A Model Father.
Joseph's Coat.
Coals of Fire.
Val Strange.
Old Blazer's Hero.
Hearts.
The Way of the World.
Cynic Fortune.
A Life's Atonement.
By the Gate of the Sea.
A Bit of Human Nature.
First Person Singular.
Bob Martin's Little Girl
Time's Revenges.
A Wasted Crime.
In Direst Peril.

By MURRAY and HERMAN.
One Traveller Returns. | The Bishops' Bible.
Paul Jones's Alias.

By HENRY MURRAY.
A Game of Bluff. | A Song of Sixpence.

By HUME NISBET.
'Bail Up !' | Dr. Bernard St. Vincent.

By ALICE O'HANLON.
The Unforeseen. | Chance ? or Fate ?

By GEORGES OHNET.
Dr. Rameau.
A Last Love.
A Weird Gift.

By Mrs. OLIPHANT.
Whiteladies.
The Primrose Path.
The Greatest Heiress in England.

By Mrs. ROBERT O'REILLY.
Phœbe's Fortunes.

By OUIDA.
Held in Bondage.
Strathmore.
Chandos.
Idalia.
Under Two Flags.
Cecil Castlemaine's Gage
Tricotrin.
Puck.
Folle Farine.
A Dog of Flanders.
Pascarel.
Signa.
Princess Napraxine.
In a Winter City.
Ariadne.
Friendship.
Two Lit. Wooden Shoes.
Moths.
Bimbi.
Pipistrello.
A Village Commune.
Wanda.
Othmar.
Frescoes.
In Maremma.
Guilderoy.
Ruffino.
Syrlin.
Santa Barbara.
Two Offenders.
Ouida's Wisdom, Wit, and Pathos.

By MARGARET AGNES PAUL
Gentle and Simple.

By C. L. PIRKIS.
Lady Lovelace.

By EDGAR A. POE.
The Mystery of Marie Roget.

By Mrs. CAMPBELL PRAED
The Romance of a Station.
The Soul of Countess Adrian.
Outlaw and Lawmaker.
Christina Chard

By E. C. PRICE.
Valentina.
The Foreigners.
Mrs. Lancaster's Rival.
Gerald.

By RICHARD PRYCE.
Miss Maxwell's Affections.

TWO-SHILLING NOVELS—continued.

By JAMES PAYN.

Bentinck's Tutor.
Murphy's Master.
A County Family.
At Her Mercy.
Cecil's Tryst.
The Clyffards of Clyffe.
The Foster Brothers.
Found Dead.
The Best of Husbands.
Walter's Word.
Halves.
Fallen Fortunes.
Humorous Stories.
£200 Reward.
A Marine Residence.
Mirk Abbey.
By Proxy.
Under One Roof.
High Spirits.
Carlyon's Year.
From Exile.
For Cash Only.
Kit.
The Canon's Ward.
The Talk of the Town.
Holiday Tasks.
A Perfect Treasure.
What He Cost Her.
A Confidential Agent.
Glow-worm Tales.
The Burnt Million.
Sunny Stories.
Lost Sir Massingberd.
A Woman's Vengeance.
The Family Scapegrace.
Gwendoline's Harvest.
Like Father, Like Son.
Married Beneath Him.
Not Wooed, but Won.
Less Black than We're Painted.
Some Private Views.
A Grape from a Thorn.
The Mystery of Mirbridge.
The Word and the Will.
A Prince of the Blood.
A Trying Patient.

By CHARLES READE.

It is Never Too Late to Mend.
Christie Johnstone.
The Double Marriage.
Put Yourself in His Place.
Love Me Little, Love Me Long.
The Cloister and the Hearth.
The Course of True Love.
The Jilt.
The Autobiography of a Thief.
A Terrible Temptation.
Foul Play.
The Wandering Heir.
Hard Cash.
Singleheart and Doubleface.
Good Stories of Men and other Animals.
Peg Woffington.
Griffith Gaunt.
A Perilous Secret.
A Simpleton.
Readiana.
A Woman-Hater.

By Mrs. J. H. RIDDELL.

Weird Stories.
Fairy Water.
Her Mother's Darling.
The Prince of Wales's Garden Party.
The Uninhabited House.
The Mystery in Palace Gardens.
The Nun's Curse.
Idle Tales.

By AMELIE RIVES.
Barbara Dering.

By F. W. ROBINSON.
Women are Strange. | The Hands of Justice.

By JAMES RUNCIMAN.
Skippers and Shellbacks. | Schools and Scholars.
Grace Balmaign's Sweetheart.

By W. CLARK RUSSELL.

Round the Galley Fire.
On the Fo'k'sle Head.
In the Middle Watch.
A Voyage to the Cape.
A Book for the Hammock.
The Mystery of the 'Ocean Star.'
The Romance of Jenny Harlowe.
An Ocean Tragedy.
My Shipmate Louise.
Alone on a Wide Wide Sea.

By GEORGE AUGUSTUS SALA.
Gaslight and Daylight.

By JOHN SAUNDERS.
Guy Waterman. | The Lion in the Path.
The Two Dreamers.

By KATHARINE SAUNDERS.
Joan Merryweather.
The High Mills.
Heart Salvage.
Sebastian.
Margaret and Elizabeth.

By GEORGE R. SIMS.

Rogues and Vagabonds.
The Ring o' Bells.
Mary Jane's Memoirs.
Mary Jane Married.
Tales of To-day.
Dramas of Life.
Tinkletop's Crime.
Zeph.
My Two Wives.
Memoirs of a Landlady.
Scenes from the Show.
The 10 Commandments.

By ARTHUR SKETCHLEY.
Match in the Dark.

By HAWLEY SMART.
Without Love or Licence.

By T. W. SPEIGHT.
The Mysteries of Heron Dyke.
The Golden Hoop.
Hoodwinked.
By Devious Ways.
Back to Life.
The Loudwater Tragedy.
Burgo's Romance.
Quittance in Full.
A Husband from the Sea

By ALAN ST. AUBYN.
A Fellow of Trinity.
The Junior Dean.
Master of St. Benedict's
To His Own Master.
Orchard Damerel.

By R. A. STERNDALE.
The Afghan Knife.

By R. LOUIS STEVENSON.
New Arabian Nights. | Prince Otto.

By BERTHA THOMAS.
Cressida.
Proud Maisie.
The Violin-Player.

By WALTER THORNBURY.
Tales for the Marines. | Old Stories Retold.

By T. ADOLPHUS TROLLOPE.
Diamond Cut Diamond.

By F. ELEANOR TROLLOPE.
Like Ships upon the Sea.
Anne Furness.
Mabel's Progress.

By ANTHONY TROLLOPE.
Frau Frohmann.
Marion Fay.
Kept in the Dark.
John Caldigate.
The Way We Live Now.
The Land-Leaguers.
The American Senator.
Mr. Scarborough's Family.
Golden Lion of Granpere

By J. T. TROWBRIDGE.
Farnell's Folly.

By IVAN TURGENIEFF, &c.
Stories from Foreign Novelists.

By MARK TWAIN.
A Pleasure Trip on the Continent.
The Gilded Age.
Huckleberry Finn.
Mark Twain's Sketches.
Tom Sawyer.
A Tramp Abroad.
Stolen White Elephant.
Life on the Mississippi.
The Prince and the Pauper.
A Yankee at the Court of King Arthur.
The £1,000,000 Bank-Note.

By C. C. FRASER-TYTLER.
Mistress Judith.

By SARAH TYTLER.
The Bride's Pass.
Buried Diamonds.
St. Mungo's City.
Lady Bell.
Noblesse Oblige.
Disappeared.
The Huguenot Family.
The Blackhall Ghosts.
What She Came Through
Beauty and the Beast.
Citoyenne Jaqueline.

By ALLEN UPWARD.
The Queen against Owen.

By AARON WATSON and LILLIAS WASSERMANN.
The Marquis of Carabas.

By WILLIAM WESTALL.
Trust-Money.

By Mrs. F. H. WILLIAMSON.
A Child Widow.

By J. S. WINTER.
Cavalry Life. | Regimental Legends.

By H. F. WOOD.
The Passenger from Scotland Yard.
The Englishman of the Rue Cain.

By Lady WOOD.
Sabina.

By CELIA PARKER WOOLLEY.
Rachel Armstrong; or, Love and Theology.

By EDMUND YATES.
The Forlorn Hope.
Land at Last.
Castaway.

OGDEN, SMALE AND CO., LIMITED, PRINTERS, GREAT SAFFRON HILL, E.C.

www.ingramcontent.com/pod-product-compliance
Lightning Source LLC
Chambersburg PA
CBHW020308170426
43202CB00008B/535